LIFE STILL GOES ON!

You must read this short thrilling, incredible, adventurous, shocking, unbelievable but true story of my life.

The Lord's lovingkindnesses indeed never cease, for His compassions never fail. They are new every morning.

Therefore I have hope in Him. The Lord is good to those who wait for Him, to the person who seeks Him.

(Lamentations 3:22-26)

LIFE STILL GOES ON

CURTIS L. HAYES

B.A. - Morningside College
M.A. - Arizona State University
Th. M. - Dallas Theological Seminary

iUniverse, Inc.
Bloomington

Life Still Goes On

iUniverse books may be ordered through booksellers or by contacting:

iUniverse
1663 Liberty Drive
Bloomington, IN 47403
www.iuniverse.com
1-800-Authors (1-800-288-4677)

ISBN: 978-1-4759-7380-8 (sc)
ISBN: 978-1-4759-7381-5 (ebk)

Library of Congress Control Number: 2013901854

Printed in the United States of America

iUniverse rev. date: 05/10/2013

CONTENTS

INTRODUCTION

"Know what you are going to say before you speak, plant your feet solidly on the floor, one foot slightly ahead of the other, do not shuffle from foot to foot as if you are scared half to death, use gestures out and away from your body, move a step or two forward or to the sides only to emphasize an important point and do not forget that personal eye contact with your audience . . ."

These were some of my instructions to the hundreds of speech students that I had the privilege to teach. My tenure as a public school teacher, pastor, missionary to Liberia in West Africa, and even as a present substitute teacher in the Roswell Independent School District will be included in the following pages of the book.

I am writing this book to the general public, and especially to my family who I love dearly. Several years ago, my life was full of anger, resentment and bitterness.

I thought about writing a book about accusations and blaming others for my dilemma without any evidence whatsoever. God's grace and mercy led me to turn this crisis in my life into an opportunity to write my story, "Life Still Goes On!" Some Biblical scriptures will be used but only for my personal references. With God's deliverance to forgive and forget (Col 3:13-17) I can now write boldly and optimistically, "For now I know that all things work together for good to them who love God and to them who are called according to His purpose," Romans 8:28.

I am grateful to God who allowed me to be:

1. The first African American to teach at the secondary level in Sioux City, Iowa Independent School District in 1956.

2. The first African American awarded a certificate and a gold plaque for being "College Orator of the year at Morningside College, Sioux City, Iowa in 1956.

3. The first African American to teach in the Highland, California Unified School System in 1961.

4. The first African American to coach the Forensics of Speech and Debate at Indio High School in Indio, California in 1967.

5. The first African American to be the President of the Desert Sands Teacher's Association in Indio, California in 1972.

6. The first African American to be a missionary in Monrovia, Liberia in West Africa with the Sudan Interior Mission in 1980.

Needless to say, I thank the Lord for these matchless experiences. The first of the Hayes' family to get a college degree and two Master degrees, one from Arizona State University and the other from Dallas Theological Seminary.

I probably, without even thinking about it until just recently, started a ripple in the Hayes' family that has not stopped. The family members and their educational achievements will be forthcoming in the book.

As President Barak Obama would say, "Now is the time, now is the time!" "We cannot wait! We cannot wait". I cannot wait either until my book, Life Still Goes On, is published.

That's why "I'm pressing on the upward bound, new heights I'm gaining every day. Still praying as I'm onward bound, Lord, plant my feet on higher ground! (song).

Certainly He's doing that—Praise His name!

I trust you will enjoy reading my life story as I have thoroughly enjoyed writing it.

Love ya,!!

Curtis

DEDICATION

To my wife, Frances, who could do most anything the twelve years that I have known her. She was diagnosed with a severe illness last year. Thank you, Lord, for allowing her to see the completion of this story of my life. It has been a difficult time, to be sure, during these past several months.

We know, however, "that Jesus Christ is our hope", I Tim 1:1.

Prayerfully,

Curtis

PROLOGUE

"Life Still Goes On", by Curtis L. Hayes, is an extra-ordinary true story of my life. A father, grandfather, and great grandfather; born to Otis and Janie Hayes in Glasgow, Missouri on January 10, 1931.

The first twenty years of my life will be discussed as I grew up in Sioux City, Iowa. We will then make our way to Lincoln University in Jefferson City, Missouri, and excitingly, we will board the USS Randall Aircraft Carrier to Seoul, South Korea,

Flying back across the ocean, we will stop briefly in Oklahoma City, Oklahoma to chat about injustices that flabbergasted me. I became a little prejudiced at this time. Wow!!

We will take trips to San Bernardino and Indio, California where I taught school for several years. What a tremendous blessing this was! My call to the ministry as I studied at the prestigious, elite, world renowned Dallas Theological Seminary.

Living in Liberia, West Africa during a recent coup d'état was very fascinating but dangerous as I was nearly shot by soldiers on two occasions. What a scary time that was!

Visiting Amsterdam in the Netherland and Paris, France were thrilling excitements. Coming back to America after spending five years on foreign soil and pastoring four United Methodist Churches stretched my faith immeasurably!

Finally, my divorce after being married for 48 years came to an end. My children and many of my relatives disowned me and thought I was being deluded by satanic demons.

I am now 81 years old, doing pretty good for myself, and trusting God to work out all things which He will do. Life Still Goes On!

Enjoy reading my life story, an incredible, thrilling, non-fiction, authentic, precise, unbelievable, but a true auto-biographical story of my life.

Prayerfully submitted,

Curtis L. Hayes

CHAPTER ONE
MY IMMEDIATE FAMILY

My name is Curtis L. Hayes, and I was born to Otis and Janie Hayes in Glasgow, Missouri on January 10, 1931. I have one older brother, Otis Jr. and a younger sister, Edna Pearline. My mother and father moved to Sioux City, Iowa when we were yet in elementary school, so I do not remember too much, if anything about Glasgow. One lane dirt roads were prevalent, and if a car was approaching, someone would have to stop and get over to let the other car go by. The hills, much like a roller coaster, were fun to ride up and down the country roads. Blacks and whites and a few Native Americans seemed to have gotten along quite well during those days. I have gone back to Glasgow a time or two, but I vaguely remember any of my uncles, aunts or cousins.

My mother and father moved to Iowa for better working conditions, better housing, and a quality education for my brother, sister and myself. My parents really worked tediously, sometimes walking to and from work to enable and provide enough financial assistance to send their three children to school dressed cleanly. I praise God for their determination, dedication and persistence to sacrifice everything for their children. Both of my parents went to be with the Lord in 1982, six months apart, after being married for 57 years.

All three of us, my brother, sister and I, went on to higher education and were superior supervisors in our professions.

My brother, Otis, was the intellectual one in the family. He maintained nearly an "A" average through high school. He had a knack for studying. He enjoyed it! He could understand Chemistry, Physics,

Geometry, Trigonometry and Calculus. I am very proud of my brother. Pearline and I would just look at each other as if to say, "Some have it and some do not." We would just laugh and go to the front porch to dance "The Jitterbug".

Otis graduated from Central High School in Sioux City, Iowa in 1947. He then went to work for Armour and Co. Packinghouse stunning cattle in the head on the beef floor. It did not take him too long to decide that this job was not for him. He went to work  as a meat inspector in St. Louis, Missouri, Ottumwa, Iowa, Chicago, IL, and retired in Athens, GA after 35 years as a government employee. He has a BA degree from Roosevelt University in Chicago, IL. His government position was interrupted briefly, as he was called and sent to Uruguay, Argentina and Brazil in South America to teach about salt, nitrite, nitrate, phosphorous and other sodium acids found in meat. He was a wizard chemist and spoke Spanish fluently, so he had no problem conversing with the people there. This definitely was an experience in his life that he will never forget. He and his wife, Delores celebrated their 60th wedding anniversary in 2010. They now live in Omaha, Nebraska where he really likes the cold weather (smile). They have three grown daughters, Karen, Kimberly, and Kristie.

My sister, Pearline, has always been pretty, tall, and very graceful, kind-hearted and just as sweet as she can be. She was a little spoiled, because she was the only girl in the family. She did not take that for granted, however, she was just Pearline. We were very close as youngsters and would always be together. As a pre-teenager, she started taking piano lessons and before she became a teenager, she could play most anything. She even played for the Mt. Zion Baptist Church choir when she was just a teenager for several years. We used to walk to elementary school, junior high school, and high school together every morning. After school, she had to walk home with friends as I went to football practice. We looked so much alike that some people thought we were twins.

Pearline was a government employee as a supervisor in the Rice Department. She had an annual check-up about 10 years ago. Her doctor told her that she was in excellent condition. That same day, she had a massive stroke which paralyzed the left side of her body and left her speech unutterable. I drove to Kansas City, Missouri to see her when she was in the hospital. The rest of the family was there and we prayed together. This certainly was a downtime for the family. We know that there is a reason for everything, and we know that God allows certain things to people who love Him. Pearline really loved God; she's always been that way! I always thank God for my sister and pray for her every day. She is now using a wheelchair to get around, but she still has that faith in God that one day she will walk again.

Pearline received her BA from Rockhurst College in 1982 and an MA in 1994 from Webster's University both in Kansas City, Missouri. Her husband, Bob, should have been the first African American to umpire baseball in the major leagues; but it just was not the right time! They reside in Kansas City, Missouri, and have two grown children, Bobette and Byron. Out of 300,000 business women, Pearline was the recipient of "Business Woman of the Year!" She went to Washington DC to receive her award. This was a great moment in her life, and something that she definitely would not forget. What a blessing! What an experience! I am very proud of my sister as well. Both my brother and sister have experienced life to the fullest!

My three children are three blessed children. Janice, our oldest, was born August 16, 1953 in Sioux City, Iowa. She was a pretty, vivacious little baby and she was certainly a joy to be around, especially in high school when I was her Speech Coach. There's one thing about Janice that everyone remembers and this is her laugh. Boy, could she laugh; you could hear her all across the campus. The students would say, "Here comes Janice." They could tell by her loud laughter.

3

Janice, even though I was her father, always called me Mr. Hayes in class. This certainly speaks highly of her character. She could have easily called my "Daddy" and gotten away with murder in class, but she did not. All her peers really loved Janice; she was a likeable person, very out-going, very friendly and just as sweet as she could be.

She was an "excellent" speaker too. She was on the Speech Squad for four years and did exceptionally well. She was also in Drama where she starred in "A Raisin in the Sun." She was one of the best well-rounded speakers I had. She would feel so badly if she did not make it to the final round. That was few and far between, because she did make it to the final round more often than not in Impromptu, extemporaneous, original oratory, Humorous and Dramatic interpretation speaking. She was also an excellent debater and was pretty good at the pros and cons of argumentation. She was a joy to watch during competition. She was also a high school cheerleader when I announced the football games over the loud-speaker. These were great memories for me, and I will never forget them. She graduated from Indio High School in 1974. Then, off to UCLA in Los Angeles where she was the Bruin Mascot, "Josephine". I remember during the games, she would come up to where I was and sit on my lap with that funny outfit she wore. She graduated from UCLA and began teaching high school for several years in Moreno Valley, California. She ultimately ventured out into the Real Estate arena. She does a little substitute teaching now, as well as preaching God's Word bi-monthly with her husband, David. They reside in Bullhead City, Arizona. They have four children: Monica, David Jr., Timothy, and Eric. More about them later!

Curtis Jr. is our middle child, born November 26, 1956 in Sioux City, Iowa. God gave us him on Thanksgiving Day. With all of the turkey, ham, mashed potatoes, collard and mustard greens, giblet gravy, candied yams, cranberry sauce, hot dinner rolls, pumpkin pies and cherry cobblers; Curtis came to be with us.

As a baby, he had eczema, a skin rash that caused him to scratch unmercifully. I felt so sorry for him. We took him to dermatologists and they prescribed ointment of one kind or another which absolutely did no good. He broke out with hives all over his face, and he would scratch and scratch until he would bleed. It was awful, to say the least. We would buy splints and tape them around his elbows, so he could not scratch. This must have gone on for at least a year. We know that God has His time-table, and eventually Curtis was healed from that itchy condition to become a normal boy. Then asthma hit him. He must have inherited that from me, because I had asthma myself as a young teenager until I went into the US Army at 19 years of age. Because of the cold winters and hot, humid days in Sioux City, Iowa, I said, "We had better go west to a hot, dry climate. We moved to San Bernardino, California in 1961.

When Curtis Jr. was in the 6th grade, he developed a kidney disease call numerilo-nephritus, which affected his urine disposal. He could not get rid of this albumen in his body. This was a very rare disease, with no cure; people usually died with it. Doctors were summoned all over California. People were praying all over California.

Cortisone was the only medication prescribed for this rare disease. Cortisone caused Curtis to swell from head to toe. His face became so round and full of fluid that I hardly recognized my own son. His arms and legs were just flabby, and I could barely see his eyes because of his swollen face. We prayed earnestly and fervently and God heard our cry and delivered miraculously Curtis back to his normal life style; but he was very sickly from the day he was born until about 13 years of age.

He was somewhat behind his peers, but he managed to be a tough catcher in a pony-league baseball team in Indio, California. He even pitched a time or two, but did not fare very well doing that.

Now, that his elephant hump body was gone, he entered Indio High School as a freshman. He did not take Speech the first year, but he did the second year. He was still a little shy, so I put him in Oratorical Interpretation, a speech already written by the likes of "I Have a Dream" by Dr. Martin L. King Jr., "Blood, Sweat and Tears" by Winston Churchill, "A Call to Arms" by Patrick Henry. Memorization of these speeches had to be done. Playing the part of the writer was what it was all about. He did well, but still, would not let himself go completely, so I put him in Dramatic Interpretation. We cut out speeches from "A

Raisin in the Sun", "Porgy and Bess", and some others. He really got into this category and did very well every time he competed. He and Janice became very close at this time competing against each other. They were both top speakers and were very faithful in their practices and successful in competition.

Curtis and Marilyn have three children: Brian, Myra and Curtis III. He is now re-married and lives in Garland, Texas with his second wife. He graduated from Dallas Baptist University with a BA and recently received an MA in Religion. He is now going through candidacy to become a licensed minister in the UMC. Praise God. I'm very proud of them! We used to travel during the summer months through the Black Hills of South Dakota and Yellowstone National Park in Wyoming. Seeing Mt. Rushmore and the gigantic volcano erupt every so often was thrilling to see by each of us. We had similar clothing that we wore as a family. People traveling would notice our blue and while and/or black and red outfits we used to wear while vacationing. People would complement us on how nice we looked.

Well, 10 years later, here comes another son, Collin, born November 21, 1966 in San Bernardino. He was a cute, plump little baby who was quite spoiled. This, of course, came naturally because he had two older siblings who were able to take care of him, Janice (13 years) and Curtis Jr. (10 years). Collin took his first baby steps when he was 9 months old at 1173 Trenton Street in San Bernardino, California. One day in the backyard, he just got up and started walking. Collin was in San Bernardino recently and took a picture of the house on Trenton Street. I'm waiting to see that picture!

As a young boy of 6 or 7 years old, he could really draw. He would draw racing cars and airplanes, then color them with beautiful colors. They looked so real I was waiting for them to move (smile). He would also draw cartoons of Mickey Mouse, Snoopy, and the Seven Dwarfs, colored them to look real. He was so good at that that I thought he would eventually become an artist, but that slowly changed. He could also hit a baseball when he was about the same age. I would pitch him tennis balls and he would hit that thing at least a half of a block. I thought he would grow up to become a baseball player, but that soon changed also.

We moved to Indio, California when he was about 10 months old. We bought a house that had a 15'x30' swimming pool in the backyard. One morning I was on my way to work, and would you believe that while Collin was riding his tricycle around the pool, he fell in? I had to jump in with all my clothes on to pull him out! We did not travel much with Collin as we did with Janice and Curtis Jr. The reason being I was very involved with my speech activities and practically every weekend I was off to some speech tournament somewhere.

As a young man, Collin married a girl named Yolanda and they had a baby girl named Chanta'l. After their divorce, Collin was working, going to school, and trying to raise Chanta'l. This was too much for him so he and Chanta'l moved in with us in Lubbock, Texas when I first started pastoring. He worked at Dillard's while pursuing his education at Texas Tech University where he received his BS in Political Science and Economics. He wanted so desperately to be a lawyer, so off he went to the Thurgood Marshall Law School in Houston, Texas while leaving Chanta'l with us for several years.

He graduated from law school and married a lawyer, Adrienne, from South Carolina. After graduating they moved to West Virginia and Collin started working at the Federal Trade Commission in Washington, DC for a couple of years. They later moved to Dallas, Texas. He has established his own law firm now, an attorney with Nikon Cell-phone in Finland where he goes once in a while and teaches International Law at Richardson Community College. He and Adrienne reside in Richardson, Texas. They have two children: Aiden and Athena. They are doing very well. I'm the proud father of three wonderful children: Janice, Curtis Jr., and Collin.

I have always been, and still am, inspired by their faith in God. They are very precious in the sight of the Lord (Psalm 116:15), and have helped me to better understand to trust God and not to put your confidence in man (Psalm 118:8). I had committed each of them to the Lord at a very young age. I am not ashamed of all of the trouble, heart-ache and pain we have all gone through, "for I know whom I believe and am persuaded that God is able to keep that which I have committed unto Him until the Day of Judgment" (II Timothy 1:12).

The previous pages were all about my immediate family. My mother, father, brother, sister, and my three (3) children are with me right now as I write happily (Psalm 144:15); my story, "Life Still Goes On!"

"He that handleth a matter wisely shall find good; and whoso trusteth in the Lord, happy is he." (Proverbs 16:20).

CHAPTER TWO
GROWING UP IN SIOUX CITY, IOWA

We lived in a two-story house at 616 Panoah Street, a few minutes away from our elementary school, Hopkins. We would walk across busy W. 7th Street, passing Thompson's Drug Store, then on to Hopkins Grade School only one-half a block away. I remember one day I was on my way to school, and I heard several rats roaming around in a trash can we had in the backyard. I found the lid and put it on the garbage can; I then found some big nails and a hammer and put several holes in the top. Then, I poured several buckets of water into the can. Later that day, I emptied the can, and all the rats had drowned. I even laugh about that sometimes.

Someone asked me one day who my role models were when I was growing up in Sioux City. I thought for a while and said, "First of all were my elementary school teachers:

Ms. Hotchfield, my kindergarten teacher. She was in her late 50's or early 60's, gray haired, tall and very nice. She was so intimately involved with every child that she would carry us to our mats and lay us down gently. She would remind us to be quiet and go to sleep. I learned to respect her sweet disposition and demeanor. She loved every child as I can remember as if we were her own children.

Ms. Dempster, first grade teacher. I was Ms. Dempster's pet for some reason. I remember she took me home with her one weekend to North Dakota where she was from. Her mother and father were living there. I rode those little Shetland ponies all around the ranch. I really hated to leave her class, because she kind of spoiled me a little bit. Ms. Dempster was in her late 20's or early 30's, very pretty, gracious and kind.

Ms. Kennedy, second grade teacher. Ms. Kennedy was in her late 40's or early 50's, short and somewhat plump. She was a good teacher who was strict. I really learned to behave in her class because she would send you to the principal's office which was just down the hall.

Ms. Durlin, third grade teacher. She was probably in her middle or late 40's, very tall and graceful who dressed neatly every day. She was a very good teacher also. She used to walk around the room, up and down the aisles to see if we were doing the work right. She was very interested in our knowing what we were doing.

Ms. Shulkin was a Jewish lady who taught the fourth grade. She was somewhat short, in her late 40's and would let you know who is in charge here? She used to walk around too to make sure we were paying attention to her instructions. I learned to really buckle down to study in her class. She would also send you to the office if you misbehaved.

Ms. Lamar, fifth grade teacher. She was a tall brunette, dressed very well all the time. She was in her late 40's, very pretty and had an air of sophistication about her. She was a type of teacher who knew exactly what she was doing. She would always remind us of the 6th grade and what to expect. She did an excellent job in preparing us for the next level.

Ms. Eyers, Junior 6th teacher, was in her late 50's or early 60's. She was a middle age woman, who was very nice and kind too. I remember more of Ms. Eyers' book, "The Wonderful Electric Elephant". She read this story to her classes every year. The book was old and most of the pages had come loose, but were held together by several rubber bands. It was a little hilarious, but this was her story to be read.

Ms. Danielson, Senior 6th teacher was a graceful woman in her 60's who always reminded us to be respectful and diligent in our studies as we prepared to go to West Junior High School.

I cannot say enough about all of these elementary teachers. There was not a mean bone in any of them. They were all very good teachers, mainly because they knew their subjects well and loved every student.

Mr. Fitzgerald was our principal, very stern, thin with white hair. He was about 60, carried a rubber hose around with him about 18" in length. He would give a couple of hits when we were sent to the office.

Our custodian was Mr. Milner who was in his 50's. He always kept the halls clean and spotless. He was always busy emptying trash, cleaning windows and everything that needed to be done. All of the children really liked him a lot.

It was at Hopkins Grade School when I learned that I could run pretty fast. We often competed against other elementary schools in the district. I even won the 100 and 200 yard dashes sometimes. It was a lot of fun. I was even given a red ribbon for winning.

I remember my sister Pearline and I joined the Mt. Zion Baptist Church and were baptized the same evening. On special days, such as Thanksgiving, Christmas and Easter, all the children would be given some literature to read. For some reason, I always memorized mine. Sometimes they were quite lengthy, at least one page long, sometimes two pages. People used to tell me that I was going to be a preacher some day. The thought never did enter my mind, but I did become a preacher later in life. I always loved to speak, and by the way, I still do.

Up the hill to West Junior High School we trudged. It is rather a mystery to me that I can remember all of my elementary teachers, but only two in junior high. I can visualize the gym coach but not his name. He used to let us rip and run, playing basketball, volleyball, ping-pong, tennis and turning flips. We would go outside sometimes and play softball and/or football. The coach was very nice.

I took a speech class from a teacher whose name I forgot, but I believe it was her ingenuity and advice that led me to venture out into the speech field.

What I do remember and never will forget the signs and the yells of the student body, "Here comes the Hayes dancing twins!" Most of the students thought that we were actually twins, but we were not. We only dressed alike when we danced. Pearline and I used to enter the yearly talent show. We could really jitterbug wearing our brown and gold or black and green outfits! We were really sharp and won first place every year for four years.

I played on a summer playground softball team when I pitched most of the time, but also caught once in a while. Adolph Lee and Sunny Favors used to pitch both who were pretty wild at times and had me running to the backstop more often than not. I also pitched horseshoes quite a bit and won first place in a tournament one year. I received another red ribbon at the time.

More role models included Hank Houston, Otis Hayes, Bernard Hubbard, Art Jackson, William Jackson, Orville Johnson, Ersel "Sam" Hayes, Wayman Williams, Bobby Green, Russell Banks, Joe Davis, Neil

Hubbard, and Poodle Lou Hayes. Undoubtedly, there were others, but these were some great horseshoe pitchers.

I remember walking to Hubbard's Ball Park on the North side of town about 5 miles from where I lived on Center Street. The Sioux City Ghosts, a Black softball team dramatized a "slow pitch" ball game. It was really fun to watch. People from neighboring cities 10-15 miles away used to come to Sioux City to watch this dramatic and hilarious game. The crowd stayed on their feet and applauded tumultuously every play. The fast ball game was usually played before the "slow pitch" game. I still remember those games as if they happened yesterday. What a memoir!!

There were some excellent home-run hitters. LJ Favors, Bill Davis, Chappy and Arnold "Shug" Davis led the way!! Bernard Hubbard, Joe Davis, Frankie Williams and Poodle Lou Hayes were the pitchers. Sammy Davis was one of the best short stops to play the game. Reginald Williams, Clayton, Vivian, and JC Johnson played in the outfield. Most of these players have now gone on to be with the Lord, but they were tremendous role-model for me. I have never forgotten them!

Horseshoe pitching was what all the guys did in Sioux City. I can't believe how good they were. They could even throw double-ringers most of the time. I believe Hank Houston was the best followed closely by Otis Hayes, Bernard Hubbard, Orville Johnson, Joe Davis, Neil Hubbard, Bobby Green, Russell Banks, Art Jackson, William Jackson, Poodle Lou Hayes, and even me, Curtis L. Hayes. We were all very good—very good horseshoe pitchers. I vividly remember all of them. Ersel "Sam" Hayes, who recently went to be with the Lord, was also an outstanding horseshoe pitcher.

Academically, I didn't do too well in high school. The Speech teacher seemingly didn't have room for me on his speech squad, so I lost a little interest. Geometry was my dilemma; I had to take the course all over again in summer school. What a drag that was, but I made it!

Football and track were the only two things which kept me going. I lettered in both sports during high school. I played quarter-back and played at defensive safety at times.

Willie Lee, James "Slick" Daniels, Rudy Lee, Ersel "Sam" Hayes, Otis Hayes, Orville Johnson and Russell Banks helped Central High School win honors for several years. We were coached by Coach McLarnan. He brought out the best in his players. I also remember Wally Piper and Doug Watland, Walt Brousard, guys who also were good football players. Walking down to Gilman Terrace after school, changing into our football gear, practicing and showering; then walking home about three miles away, we were worn out by the time we got home, but it was fun. I would do it all over again!!

There were a couple of boys from Lemars, Iowa (Gunther and Pew) who ran track, and boy, could they run! Central High School also had two guys who could really run (Willie Lee and Slick Daniels). When the 100 and 200 yard dashes were to be run and those four guys were in the race, the crowd just went crazy. The time keepers had to be at their best because the four of them were always so close at the finish line. Sometimes the time keepers had to get together to see who won by a split second.

I could not compete against then, so my best bet was running the 200 in a medley relay. I tried the low hurdles and pole vault, but I was never that competitive.

My brother Otis was a quarter-miler. One day in the Sioux City relays, he was running against some of the best in the State. The gun sounded and 8 to 10 runners were speeding around the track. Otis was leading the pack. About three quarters of the way around, Otis starting slowing down. He was running out of gas! I believe he came in next to last. I laugh about that sometimes. It was funny, but not funny, because I wanted to see my brother win . . . I'll never forget that track meet—seems like yesterday!

I was a 1949 mid-term graduate from Central High School. After that, I worked for Armour's Packing house on the beef floor shackling cattle. My brother, Otis use to hit the cattle in the head and roll them out on the floor to Henry Atkins and me. We would put shackles around their ankles and hoist them up on a rail to be sent to Tebow, Mr. Zook and others who slit their throats and skinned the hide off their heads. I often think of the many cattle that were thought to be dead would get up and run all over the beef floor. I remember "Stretch, Mr. Daniels, Mr. Winfrey, Charlie Hancock, William Jackson, Art Jackson, as well as others, used to run to get out of the way. It was funny then, but not funny, because I did not want to see anybody get hurt. We used to holler up at Otis, Kill em! Kill em; kill em Otis! He thought they were dead. "Yeah, right!"

There was a man who moved to Sioux City in the mid 50's. I cannot remember his name to save my neck, but he sure could play a tenor sax.

I had always been interested in playing a saxophone. I asked him if he would teach me, and he said that he would. I bought a C-melody sax at a pawn shop and began my lessons. I caught on pretty fast, playing such songs as "Mary had a little lamb, Jingle bells and Here Comes Santa". I would take these "nursery rhymes and "jive" them up while playing "Kansas City, Here I Come". That was the song then!

I do not recall my debut at the 51 Club on W. 7th Street during the mid 50's, but I do remember playing with CK Kenner and Reginald Williams on the trumpet, Nate Lee on the bass, Harry Smith on the piano, Ashunel Bizzet on the drums and this other man and me playing the sax. The enormous crowds would holler, "Blow Curt, Blow Curt". This was a great memoir, but it did not last long. I got tired of making the trips to Omaha, Nebraska because more often than not, we did not get back to Sioux City until the "wee" hours in the morning; and I had to be at work at 6:00 AM. Ultimately, I gave my C-melody sax away. It was like saying good-bye to a long-time friend. The sax was coming between my wife, my two small children and me. I was spending too much time with it and not with them. So, I gave it up! Sometimes in life you have to give up what seems to be good for you.

CHAPTER THREE
LIFE STILL GOES ON!

During the summer of 1950, I met a girl about 14 years of age from Bartlesville, Oklahoma who had come to Sioux City to visit relatives. She was very cute and dainty. You have heard the saying many times, "it was love at first sight". We started a boyfriend-girlfriend relationship that summer. She went back to Newkirk, Oklahoma where her family had recently moved. She only lived two blocks away from a high school, but she had to ride a school bus 14 miles one way to Douglas High School in Ponca City, Oklahoma. How awful! I had previously enrolled at Lincoln University in Jefferson City, Missouri. We corresponded with each other by mail the following year.

I caught a train in Sioux City for Kansas City, Missouri. I was to change trains in Kansas City. Unfortunately, I missed the first train going to Jefferson City because I was afraid to ask someone what gate I had to go to. At that time in my life, I was very shy. The first time away from my family and being around so many black people was new to me. My mother told me when I left, "Now, you be careful and watch your money!" I was too careful, too careful to find the train to Jefferson City. Finally, another train came, and I made it to the Capital City, Jefferson City, Missouri.

Lincoln University was a prestigious school, situated high upon a hill, very gigantic looking from the bottom of the hill. A Black university with all black professors and an all black student body was really awesome to me. I loved it from the beginning. I met a lot of nice people from different states during my year at Lincoln University.

Football was the main attraction at Lincoln. When there was a home football game, people from nearby cities would come. The stadium would be packed. When there were no more tickets to be sold because of seating problems, people had to stand on the outside of the chain link fence to see the game or watch it from the top of the hill. It was something to behold!

The football teams, bands, majorettes and cheerleaders would all come in their beautiful colors. I mean they were sharp-dressed up!! I had never seen anything near like this in my life. I was really excited, just like a small child opening his presents on Christmas morning.

They really put on a SHOW during half-time. The bands and majorettes would really "shake it up". The crowd was frenzy; into every movement as well. It was high above what I expected, a great memoir.

It seemed as if it took hours for the stadium to clear. People just hung around after the game, eating bar-be-cue, playing music and even dancing, especially if Lincoln had won.

I had some outstanding professors at Lincoln University; it was a year of great remembrances. I pledged the Kappa Alpha Psi Fraternity, and I became a scroller or little brother as we were called. We had to carry match boxes everywhere we went. If a "Big brother" asked us for a match and if we did not have one, we would get the paddle.

I remember one evening a "Big brother" came to my room and told me to stand up in a chair and blow out a light bulb on the ceiling! Blow out a light bulb?! How ridiculous! I tried and tried but never succeeded. He came back a couple of hours later; I was still blowing! He said, "You can get down now and write me a one-page synopsis on how to blow out a light bulb. I'll be back in our hour to pick it up. This was just one of the many things our "Big brothers" had us to do.

Another occasion was when they put about 15 of us little brothers in a truck with only our underwear, drove us to Columbia, Missouri, tarred and feathered us with newspaper, tissue paper, cotton and anything else that would stick. They then told us to run all the way back to Jefferson City about 30 miles away. Needless to say, some did not make it. One boy was hit in the back and messed up his spine. I never heard the full outcome of this, because I did not return to Lincoln for my sophomore year.

I went home for the summer and received a letter from Uncle Sam that said, "I Need You!" I was inducted in the Army July 26, 1951 in

Omaha, Nebraska. It took approximately two weeks to complete the orientation. I was then taken to Ft. Leonardwood, Missouri, where I went through 16 weeks of basic training. It was pure "hell", getting up before dawn, peeling potatoes, shoveling sand, dirt and rocks, washing pots and pans, crawling through the "infiltration course" while machine gun bullets were directly above you, sleeping in tents and eating out of tin cans. This was not for me, but I was in the Army now, and you do exactly what you are told to do. I was given a US serial number to never forget; the platoon leaders would not let you forget, because periodically they would ask you, "Private, what's your serial number?" I would say, US 55-173-018. To this day, 60 years later, I have never forgotten it. I thank God for this experience for it taught me to be obedient and respectful. The Army was gracious to me, because it allowed me to receive my BA and MA degrees with monetary assistance.

Given a short furlough, I went to Newkirk, Oklahoma to say good-bye to my first love. I remember riding the train to Newkirk; the city was so small the train did not even stop to let me out. I guess they had forgotten that someone was to get off in Newkirk. One of the porters realized it and stopped the train that backed up about two blocks to let me off. The family was waiting for me to get off and was amazed when the train kept going. I was amazed too!

It was good to see my girlfriend again after a year or so. We decided to get married on Dec. 17, 1951 in Winfield, Kansas before I went to South Korea. A few days later, I went to Camp Stoneman, California and boarded the USS Randall Aircraft Carrier on January 6, 1952 to South Korea. What a drag! While I was gone for a year, my wife matriculated at Langston University in Langston, Oklahoma. Life still goes on!

The carrier steered in Seoul, South Korea, the Capital City. It was really a sad sight to see the once beautiful skyscrapers and other buildings destroyed by massive North Korean bombs. After viewing the city briefly, the hundreds of soldiers went by rail to Suwon where I would spend the next 11 months. Stepping off the train, I could easily smell the human dung. Young and old, men, women, boys and girls would pass by our barracks with somewhat of a yoke over their heads to equalize the weight of the buckets on both ends full of human dung to be used to fertilize their fields of rice, grain, wheat, barley, cassava, beans or whatever they had planted. While writing, I am reminded of Matthew 11:30 who says, "My yoke is easy and my burden is light." The South Koreans took their work in stride; they used to sing while they worked, they seem to be enjoying it. This was their culture; this was what they had to do to survive. We in America would think it was a burden; it probably would be for us but not to them.

Most of the people I saw in Suwon worked somewhere; I saw no beggars on the streets while I was there. I remember the hot summer days, much like it is in Roswell, NM at 105° today, and the cold winters much like it is in Des Moines, Iowa. I met a lot of nice people in Suwon who worked for me when I was a cook.

I ended up working in the mail room with several South Koreans under my supervision. I often think about them, they were special people in my life and were excellent workers.

Finally, my year was up but it seemed to be much longer. We flew back to the States in late December, 1952, to Oklahoma City, Oklahoma. We stopped at a bus station to get something to eat. Would you believe that they would not serve any blacks in this bus terminal? I was flabbergasted!! Guess what? We blacks were told that we had to go outside and down an alley to order what we wanted through an 8" by 12" screened in window. I said, "No way, Jóse, I will starve first."

I was in complete uniform with my Korean Service Metal, my bronze star and other citations on my lapel. After serving my country in a militarized zone in South Korea, what had I done that was so wrong to not be able to sit down and eat? I could not understand it then, I still cannot. I will never forget that ordeal, but that is the way life was then, but life still must go on.

Some white soldiers bought us some hamburgers and some French fries and we ate them on our way to Ft. Sill, Oklahoma. What a welcome home that was!! I still shake my head in disbelief. I was in Ft. Sill for a couple of weeks for medical examinations and other procedures mandatory by the Army.

My wife joined me and we went to Ft. Bliss, Texas for a few months where I was honorably discharged July 24, 1953. At this time, my wife was pregnant with our first child to be named Janice. We moved to Sioux City, Iowa in late July, 1953, where Janice was born on August 16, 1953. Before we left Ft. Bliss, I remember our having no money at the end of the month. All we had to eat until payday were some Collard and mustard greens, and my wife left the burner on too long—and burned the greens. We had nothing to eat that night. The lady in the other side of the duplex brought us something to eat. Pitiful! Pitiful!

Back in Sioux City, my wife and I enrolled at Morningside College, a small but prestigious college owned and operated administratively by the United Methodist Church. To be a small college, it was to be feared in football, basketball and baseball. Morningside College was in a conference with big schools, such as the University of South Dakota, South Dakota State, Mankato State to name just a few. This small school In comparison to the other schools was dynamite. Coaches Buckingham and Dewey Halford were two of the best. Their football and baseball teams were one of the best for several years. I remember Chuck Obye, as a player before he became the basketball coach, could really shoot from behind the arc. Today they would have been 3 points instead of 2. I used to go to most of the football and basketball games. I never liked baseball that much at that time.

Janice was only 2 months or so old when we decided to go to school. I thank God for the GI Bill which allowed us both to further our educational endeavors.

Gonzella and Candy Mae Denny, my wife's cousins took care of Janice daily during this time. As I look hindsight now, this was a tremendous sacrifice on the part of my wife to leave her baby to go back to college. This speaks very highly of her maturity; she was very smart too. We were in the same education class together and she was one of the tops in the class. I could never outscore her on our weekly exams. Life still goes on!

Dr. Frederic Howe and Dr. Jerry West were my speech professors. Dr. West was the head of the speech squad that did a little traveling to speech tournaments. He had heard me speak a few times in class, and he encouraged me to write an original oratory to compete at an upcoming tournament at the University of Nebraska in Lincoln, Nebraska. He wanted me on his squad and I desperately wanted to be on it. He told me to write on a subject that I was passionate about, a subject that is paramount in the news, write about a subject that disturbs you deeply. I thought and thought and thought some more. It was the year 1954 when the United States Supreme Court had recently handed down a decision to integrate schools in the United States. I thought about my wife and how she had to ride a school bus for 14 miles when there was a high school within walking distance. I thought about all the Black schools in the south; I thought about all of the injustices put on Blacks, not being able to eat in restaurants, not being able to attend the University of Mississippi; churches being set on fire while four little children burned. I read about the Ku Klux Klan and how they used to throw bottles and other paraphernalia on front lawns. I remember reading about Dr. Martin L. King Jr. and all that he went through. Certainly those things never should have happened! I thank God that he never fought back with evil and animosity. He fought evil with goodness in his heart. "I have a dream, he said that one day all of God's children would hold hands together (Black, White, Yellow, Brown, and Red) and walk down the streets of brotherhood."

I remember my own life as a teenager who could not eat in a downtown restaurant and another restaurant on the north side of Sioux City, Iowa. And of course my remembrance of the bus terminal in Oklahoma City, Oklahoma. The word, "INJUSTICE" came to my mind. That is it, "Injustice" "Injustice"! That is it. The word "injustice" troubled my spirit. I could not for the life of me understand why Blacks were treated so unfairly. This definitely was an injustice. What else could you call it?

I went to Dr. West and told him what I had in mind and why this subject "Injustice!" He said, "Go for it!! Curtis, Go for it!" With Dr. West's help, we sat down and put the outline together. The speech, I thought, was very powerful and a masterpiece!!

Now, HANG ON!! Life still goes on!

Dr. West, several white students who were on the speech squad and I traveled by van to Lincoln, Nebraska for the speech tournament at University of Nebraska. We were refused motel accommodations and eating facilities. To my dismay, I told myself, "What in the hell is going on!"

However, these encounters only intensified my innermost feelings. This experience seemed to give me some added ammunition as I entered the room to speak. I was ready—really ready now! I was competing against some of the best orators in the country. They came from "big" schools such as the University of Iowa, Minnesota, Wisconsin, Illinois, Nebraska, South Dakota State, North Dakota State, Kansas, Colorado, Northwestern and other places.

God was definitely with me throughout the tournament. I felt good as I spoke several rounds before the final championship round. I received a "Superior" award as all three judges were unanimous in their praise of the oration. Dr. Gilbert Rau of Central Missouri State College said this in evaluating Hayes' oration, "This was more than a mere contest speech; it was a real message. Mr. Hayes presented honest convictions in an inspired manner. This was a truly challenging oration!" What a memoir that was!

I thank the Lord for what He did, not only that day, but for what He is doing in my life right now while I write my autobiography, "Life Still Goes On!"

Before graduating from Morningside College, I had written several schools in different states applying for a teaching position. I was optimistic knowing that I was going to receive a contract somewhere. I never did!! I was disheartened! Two schools seemed to be very interested, but finally sent me a telegram telling me that they had just hired someone. It was only after they had received my credentials, recommendations and a picture of me that I was notified. The word injustice was now beginning to show its ugly face again. I could not understand it!! I still cannot fathom its rationality. I have said many times, it does not make any difference what you are going through, "Life still must go on!!

21

CHAPTER FOUR
FROM JAIL TO THE CLASSROOM

One Saturday morning in 1956, I went in a neighborhood store on the East side of Sioux City to buy a "picnic" of beer. A picnic was one big bottle that held four quarts. My money was on the counter. The man who worked there asked me, "What kind of beer do you want?"

I said, "It doesn't matter just so it's cold."

Again he said, "What kind of beer do you want?"

Again I said, "It doesn't matter just so it's cold."

He got a little huffy for no reason; my money was still on the counter. All I wanted was a cold beer. He then said, "Boy, if you were in Alabama or Georgia or Mississippi, you would not be talking to a white man the way you are. To this very day I still do not understand why the man did not sell me a picnic of beer. This man was about 6'6" and weighed I guess about 250 lbs. I was 5'6" and weighed about 135 lbs. To my knowledge no black man likes to be called Boy by a white man. I was not a boy; I had been in the Army, and to me "boy" was an insult. I was by then getting perhaps a little huffy myself. I had done a little boxing, so I was not fearful. He came out from behind the counter and was getting ready to push me out of the store. He put his hands on me! Now, he never should have done that! My mother used to tell me "if anyone hits you for no apparent reason, you pick up the first thing you can get your hands on, and you try to kill him!" I was like David fighting Goliath (I Samuel 17:4). To my surprise and to his too, I suppose, I hit him as hard as I could in his gut. He went down holding his stomach. I started stomping him in the face; I saw blood coming! My buddies

Stretch and Ross Brown said, "Get him, Curt!!! Get him, Curt! I really tried to hurt him. I was mad at white folks then anyway, because of the way I had been treated.

"Come on Curt, the cops are coming." I did not care; all I was doing was protecting myself. The police were not far away anyway, because Stueben Street on the Eastside was one of those streets the police patrolled day and night 24-7. Two policemen ran into the store; one grabbed me by the arm, I knocked his hand away and said, "I'll go anywhere you want me to go but don't touch me!! I got into the police car and went to jail where I was finger-printed and locked up for a few hours. I was bailed out shortly by some women's club. The following week I was to appear in court. The man who I had the fight with came to court carrying a big paper sack with his shirt inside that was full of blood to be used as evidence against me. The judge, however, threw the case out of court, fined me $25.00 for disorderly conduct in a place of business. I don't know who paid the $25.00, but I was free to go.

I was supposed to be given some type of recognition at the Baccalaureate ceremony for my achievement as College Orator of the year, but I could not attend this important service because I was in jail. (Smile)

The following week, the Superintendent of the Sioux City, Iowa Independent School District, Dr. Marvin T. Nodland, called me on the telephone and asked me if I could come to see him. For what, I wondered? I never applied to teach school in Sioux City. I had already applied and was accepted in Law School at the University of South Dakota in Vermillion, South Dakota. I actually thought that I wanted to be an attorney and not a school teacher.

I did go to see Dr. Nodland. He was very cordial and I was very comfortable. He started the conversation by congratulating me on my speech "Injustice" that I had given at the University of Nebraska. It was in the Sioux City Journal newspaper. I thanked him for the compliment. He then asked me, "Were you in jail last week? That was also in the newspaper. He might have thought I was going to lie; but

I said, "Yes".

He said, "For what?"

I said, "I got into a fight".

He said, "Did you win?"

I said, "Yes, I got in a lucky punch".

Then he said, "How would you like to be the first black teacher at the secondary level in our school district?" Can you imagine!? I got my first teaching position by winning a speech tournament and getting into a fight. Never once did Dr. Nodland ask me about my grades or anything like that. Unbelievable, but true.

That September in 1956, I was assigned to teach at Woodrow Wilson Junior High School on the Eastside of Sioux City, situated half way up a high hill. During the winter when snow and ice covered the street, I could not drive up the hill. I had to park my car down on 4th and Jones St. and walk the few blocks uphill to the school. I did not mind then, because I always dressed for days like this.

For the next five years, I taught Geography. History, English and was an assistant football coach.

Mr. E. E. Briggs, the principal, was one of the nicest, most disciplined principals during my tenure of 20 years as a secondary Public School teacher. Most principals in the late 50;'s and early 60's were somewhat fearful in supporting teachers. Not Mr. Briggs; he would always back up a teacher, no matter what, and I believe that this was one of the reasons that he was well-respected and liked by all the teachers at Woodrow and throughout the district.

One of my professors at Morningside College was Dr. Russell Eidsmoe. I remember him telling us about teaching and what we need to do; he went through 4 steps:

One: Seat the students in alphabetical order and get to know their names as fast as you can.

Two: Know your subject material; know what and how you are going to teach a lesson.

Three: Do not let any student tell you what they are going or not going to do. Do not take any stuff from them!

Four: Love them! Love them! Wow!! If you catch them sleeping, if they do not do their homework, if they have not read the material to be discussed, love them anyway (I Cor. 13:13)

Sixty years later, I have never forgotten those admonitions. I have always tried to follow those guidelines even as I presently substitute in the Roswell Independent School District. I cherish those memories!

I had one student at Woodrow Wilson Junior High School who refused to read a short paragraph in class. I called on him three times to read, and three times he refused. Now, what was I suppose to do? I remembered what Dr. Eidsmoe said, "Do not let any student tell you what they are going or not going to do". At this time, I had a tough decision to make. I was the only Black teacher in this 99% all white school. If I reprimanded this kid, the district probably would have fired me. So be it! My mind was on this kid; what could I do to help him? I wanted to help him to mature. This was not to be. Suppose I would have let him slide by and not read? Other students would undoubtedly do the same thing, and I could not let that happen, especially in my first year of teaching. I thank God that He did not let me allow this kid to slide. If I had, my 20 years of teaching would have gone downward instead of upward.

Ultimately, I had to send this kid out in the hall to stand. Instead, he went home or somewhere. I knew where he lived; I should have gone by his house to check on him, but I did not. I believe I did the best thing that day. Proverbs 22:6 says, "Train up a child in the way he should go and when he is old, he will not depart from it." I don't know if I succeeded or not, I never saw him again. Life still must go on!

CHAPTER FIVE
GO WEST YOUNG MAN

After five (5) years of teaching in Sioux City, my sights were set on a hot, dry climate somewhere out West. I got tired of all the snow in the winters, shoveling snow off the sidewalk and from around the car, scraping icy windows and picking up my Uncle Allen to take him to work at 5:00 A.M. I got tired of the hot humid summers and the cold winters. I got tired of seeing cornfields most of my life. It was time to venture out to somewhere different.

Janice had hay fever in the summertime and before the frost; she would sneeze and sneeze. Curtis Jr. had asthma all the time. It was time for us to leave. It was time for us to look out West for employment. I looked at several cities in California.

San Bernardino struck a musical chord that sounding like a sweet melody to my ears. California; San Bernardino, California. The sweet music never went away. I contacted the San Bernardino City School System about employment for the 61-62 school year. I heard from them within a week. I said to myself, "They sure answered fast!" They told me to report to the Curtis Motel in St. Paul, Minnesota where the interview would be held.

Minnesota? Drive 300 miles for an interview? My goodness!? Then, I thought; the climate in Sioux City is really not helping my kids, and we had never been to the State of Minnesota. The interviews were being held at the Curtis Motel and my name is Curtis, too. I thought that only the best could happen from this coincidence or perhaps, God was at work. I knew the best was yet to come!

My family and I motored to St. Paul, Minnesota and had no problem finding the Curtis Motel. The interview went extremely well with the two administrators from San Bernardino. I was offered a contract for the 61-62 school year, making more than $5,000 to what I was earning in Sioux City. I thanked them graciously for their consideration and acceptance of me that day.

We prayed and sang all the way back to Sioux City. This was certainly another high point in my life. Wow! What a memoir!

It was difficult to leave family and friends and co-workers, but it was time to move on, for time waits for no one, it keeps going on and on.

We bought a new Ford Comet Station Wagon in 1961' the first new car I ever bought.

We sold some of our furniture and gave away what we could not or did not sell. We headed west to San Bernardino, California. We were a happy family knowing that God was leading us. We passed through the State of New Mexico, and we saw all these billboard signs about tacos, enchiladas, burritos, and other Mexican foods. I was 30 years of age and had never tasted Mexican food in my life. We were nearing Las Cruces, New Mexico and we decided to stop there for some Mexican food. We enjoyed it immensely!! It was very delicious!

The very next day, we found a two-bedroom furnished duplex to rent. I was assigned to teach in Highland, California, about 12 miles from San Bernardino. That was not bad then, because gasoline was a lot cheaper than it is now. Later, we bought a cute three-bedroom house at 1173 Trenton Street. Sixteen years later we sold this house when I went to seminary.

Teacher orientation week went well at Highland Junior High School, another 99.9% white school with one girl from the Philippine Islands. I thought I was going to be assigned to a Black school on the West side of San Bernardino, but that was ok. I had just left a nearly all white school in Sioux City, so it was no big problem to me. I had been around white people all my life.

I was one of the few new teachers at Highland Junior High and everyone was very nice and welcomed me as the new Speech teacher. I was happy about that!

Opening day finally came and the students were well-dressed and well-behaved. The year 61-62 went well, but I did have a little problem with one boy as I did in Sioux City, Iowa.

This boy took more than enough time to take his seat after I had told him to do so. The principal had come into the room about the same time I told this boy to sit down. The principal was there to evaluate my teaching techniques. After the class was over, he told me to see him in his office. I did. He told me that I was a little too strict and mean and to lighten up a bit. We never did get along too well from day one.

Christmas season came around; students showered me with gifts of socks, handkerchiefs, ties, and polo shirts. I carried what I could to his office. Look at all the things the students gave me! I'm too mean, am I? I'm too strict, am I? He turned as red as a beet. He did not know what to say.

He resigned or got fired or retired, I don't know and really did not care what happened to him or where he went.

I had already asked to be transferred to a school on the Westside of San Bernardino where there were some Black kids. Not that I have anything against teaching white students, but I wanted to teach some Blacks. This was a secondary reason for leaving Iowa. Black kids have been deprived and denied for so long that I thought my expertise could be better utilized within that kind of environment. I was assigned to Franklin Junior High School, a school of nearly 600 students; 50% Black, 47% Mexican, and 3% Anglo or White. I was really excited about this opportunity and challenge.

Opening day finally came! It was love at first sight. They were nice looking kids, dressed nice and everything. They were very accepting to me, very warm and cordial. My thoughts often go back to the many students I still well-remember even to this day—some 55 years later.

Being a speech major myself in college, my whole intention was to get some of these students involved in public speaking. I know from my own personal experience that speaking will help people overcome a number of problems, as it did for me.

The high schools in the San Bernardino-Riverside area were having speech tournaments on some weekends during the school year. I wanted to desperately to get some of these students involved, however, ninth (9th) graders could not or did not participate in forensic activities. I never relinquished my idea. I never gave up! One day shortly after the beginning of school, I went to San Bernardino High School to ask the speech teacher if some of the students from Franklin Junior High school compete in the Speech tournaments. He thought they could, because these students would be going to that high school next year, so he was optimistic about it. He checked with the local National Forensic League board members. He called me a couple of days later and said that it would be OK if I wanted to compete. I was jumping up and down for this privilege, opportunity and challenge. All right now, Curt! Get them ready!! As President Barack Obama would say, "This is you time, this is your moment!"

I looked out amongst the ninth (9th) graders with their eagle-eyes and attentiveness, the girls with perms and the boys with their hair cut short. They looked good, very attractive that first week. With their smiling faces while leaning forward, they were always interested in what I was about to say.

I started this day out by saying, "How many of you would like to go to a speech tournament and speak. Only one or two raised their hand. Most of them did not even know what a speech tournament was, for they had never been to one. I then said, "I will give you an A on your report card if you participate. More of them leaned forward now. I said, "But this is what you have to do, you must come to practice every morning and every evening; memorize your speeches and believe in your heart that you can win first place. Some leaned backwards indicating that they were not too interested. Ten students were interested and wanted to give it a try. I wrote their parents to inform them what I expected and they all agreed. I told the 10 students that we would begin our sessions next Monday, three (3) days from today at 8 o'clock in the morning. One student was late, and I reminded him that if he was late again, he would not be able to participate. Unfortunately, he was late again; that left nine (9) students, who met me the following Monday morning at 8:00 a.m. I also reminded them that they must believe in themselves to win first place. If I did not believe that they were good enough to win, they would not go the first time, maybe the second time around they would be ready. They understood! Praise the Lord! They understood! Win! Win! Win! Or stay home. That was my criteria and that never changed during my 20 years as a Speech coach.

That Monday morning I went through the various speaking categories that they could enter. They were Original Oratory, Oratorical Interpretation, Oratorical Analysis, Humorous Interpretation, Dramatic Interpretation, Extemporaneous and Impromptu speaking. I explained all of these and even gave demonstrations of them. The copied them down! When you come back at 7:00 p.m., let me know what category you think is best for you. They did!! The following week during class, I would send them to the library. Ms. Barbara Cravens was very helpful in finding them speeches. We went over the speeches together carefully noting especially the author's purpose and how he/she arrived at that conclusion. Now, read about the author's life, get to know as much as you can about the author. Now, walk in his/her shoes and deliver this speech like you think they would do.

This was exciting!! Everything was coming together pretty good when I heard them read their speeches. All of their speeches "seemed to have fitted them quite well." We started practicing every morning at 8:00 a.m. and every evening at 7:00 p.m. Some were still reading their speeches, and I had to remind them again that these speeches had to be memorized. One student dropped out because he wanted to play football. That left 8 speakers!

We continued to practice and the memorization was coming slowly but surely. They were looking good! The tournament was coming up in a couple of weeks, and we were getting more excited. To get more practice outside of my classroom, I asked several teachers at Franklin if I could send some students over to practice in front of your class. The agreed whole-heartily. All 8 students did this daily for over a week. They would come back to class all eagle-eyed and bushy tailed. They were about ready to go for their first speech tournament. That final week before the tournament we met and just discussed how we felt. They were all enthusiastic and thought that they would be extremely competitive. With these smiling faces and glowing eyes, they felt very confident, relaxed and assured of doing the best that they could do. We held hands that Friday evening and prayed that God would bless us through the tournament.

"Dress sharp" I told them, "boys, wear a nice suit, white shirt and tie and do not forget to shine your shoes; girls, dress like you are going to church, no long earrings and no high heel shoes!"

That Saturday morning at 7:30 a.m., we met at the school. We got in a couple of cars and went to San Bernardino High School. We stood outside the school for a moment. I said, "All right Franklin Trojans, we have practiced hard, Get with it!" I can still see their smiling faces and haring them say, "OK, let go get then!" Wow!! What a blessing! They were sharp and ready to go.

Of the eight (8) participants, four (4) did exceptionally well, earning trophies for their endeavors; the other four (4) made it to the championship round but did not place. I was certainly a proud speech coach! Everyone at Franklin was very happy that we had done so well. Juanita Fite, Gary Kirkwood, Freddie Stuart and Reginald Brown brought home the trophies. Other finalists were Faye Sidney, Cleodis George, Johnnye James and Ezell McDowell. I sure wish that I could see them again; they were my pride and joy.

More students got involved, and the news around the district began to spread like wild-fire. Coaches were even wondering how could this school, located in a "ghetto" compete against all those high schools and do so well. Someone said, "It only takes a spark to get a fire going. And soon all those around can warm up to its glowing."

For the next several years, the fire kept going, and the students kept winning, and they warmed up to its glowing! This seemed to have been an impossible task, but God can turn impossibilities into possibilities. All the students needed was faith as a grain of mustard seed (Matthew 17:20), and nothing shall be impossible.

My good friend and co-teacher at Franklin was Larry Mahan. We became almost inseparable. We both were very involved with the students, we loved them very much. We always knew that we were the best teachers at the school, because our main concern was student achievement. I will always remember Larry; he has helped me out in so many ways. Of the 50 teachers at Franklin, most of them are now deceased. Larry keeps me informed about others as well as some students too. I can't say enough about Larry who has always stuck close to me like a brother. He certainly is a true friend indeed. He and his wife, Donna came to Roswell, New Mexico in 2009 to see me. Boy! Was I surprised?! He still looked the same as he did 45 years ago.

The ripple continues to go as I plan to leave Franklin after this school year to Indio High School in Indio, California to become their new Speech coach. It was very difficult for me to leave Franklin after we started a fire with only a spark that will keep burning and never stop.

Our family drove down to Indio one weekend to check out the city and look for a house. It was 130° when we arrived there. No one told me that it got that hot there. I started to turn around and go back to San Bernardino. Driving through the city, we noticed all the date palm trees standing at least 100 feet high. It was a beautiful sight as they lined both sides of the boulevard. We did not know at the time that Indio, California was the date capital of the nation. We also noticed orange, lemon, apples and grapefruit trees everywhere.

We were so busy noticing all of the fruit trees that we were about to run out of town. Indio is a very small city compared to San Bernardino. We turned around to look for a house to buy. A street called Stone Canyon Boulevard sounded good to us, so we drove down the three block street. The last house on the street had a for sale sign by owner on the front lawn. We stopped in to talk to the owner. He was very nice and showed us around the house; four bedrooms, a den, 2-1/2 bathrooms, a large living room, a nice size dinette room and a very nice kitchen. And, wow!! In the backyard was a 15' by 30' swimming pool. There were nine grapefruit trees around the house with a beautiful diachondra lawn that had to be mowed once every three or four months. We loved it! We gave the owner a deposit, and he said, "The house is yours!" What a blessing from God! We drove back to San Bernardino all aglow about this house that even had a 3 car garage!

School was about to close at Franklin, but I had already told them that I would be leaving them, but keep the ripple going, keep on speaking! It was a sad but happy goodbye!

CHAPTER SIX
DOWN IN THE VALLEY

We put up a for rent sign and rented the house within days. We packed up most of our furniture but left some for the lady who was going to rent the house, because she did not have much furniture. She was blessed and we were blessed as well, knowing that we had helped a widow with three (3) children.

Down in the valley we went to Indio, California the home of the date shake, a delicious, extremely thick milk shake made with dates. The city generated 95% of the dates grown and harvested in the United States.

Burl Ives used to sing, "Down in the valley, the valley so low. Hang your head over, hear the wind blow. Hear the wind blow, love, hear the wind blow. Hang your head over, hear the wind blow."

I remember driving the distance of 70+ miles down from San Bernardino to Indio and hearing the wind blow. The wind did not only blow hard, but it blew dust and sand right into the windshield. Sometimes it would be difficult to see where we were going. The sand was terrible to the point where I had to replace the windshield two or three times a year. That was our first welcome to our new home. Now, read about the second welcome. We turned onto Stone Canyon Boulevard, and noticed that there were at least five (5) houses with For Sale signs in their yards. I could not help but think that they were selling out because a Black family was moving in. I don't know why I thought that—I just did!

There were no other blacks living on this street, but so what? I bought the house because it was close to schools and shopping areas. I did not want to live out in the "boondocks" where there were no lights at night. After several months the "For Sale" signs came down, the houses were not selling for some reason. My mind went back to the word injustice. How long, how long, how long are you going to halt between two opinions (I Kings 18:21).

Eventually, we became neighborly, and read this next sentence, several of these families used our swimming pool as much as we did. What a paradox!! God works in mysterious ways, His wonders to perform.

We were led by the Holy Spirit in the first place to even be in Indio, and we know that God says in Romans 14:19, "Let us follow peace and things wherewith one may edify another." I know that I have been blessed with a talent to help bless others. For this, I'm grateful!

Indio High School had always been very competitive in Speech within their district of twenty-five (25) schools south of San Bernardino. Indio was not in the same district as San Bernardino was, so I did not know how the students from Franklin were doing.

Drama and Speech were together at Indio High. The teacher had asked me to come down to Indio to take over the Speech exclusively and he would only be involved with the drama. That sounded pretty good to me, but that was not the way it was to be.

His drama classes used to put on some excellent shows. These students were so good, that the plays were often extended for a week or two, so more people would have an opportunity to see the play. He had some "real" good actors and actresses. The drama students were also used in competitive speech. It was somewhat difficult for me to do any coaching with them, because they were usually rehearsing for a play.

I felt that many of the juniors and seniors did not want my help anyway. My ego was hurt. It's hard to change horses in the middle of a stream. I can understand that, but that will not help me. If many of the upper classes wanted their former teacher to also be their Speech coach—so be it!! So be it!! I will find my own speakers! I'll find my own!

There was a tournament coming up in San Diego, and I wanted so desperately to go. The Drama department was rehearsing for a play, so I could not use any of them. Some of the students thought, perhaps, I was a bit inexperienced, I don't know for sure. I do know that I had to do what I thought I knew I should do. By God's leading me, I knew what to do.

The media and others thought that Senator Barack Obama was inexperienced, but he has fooled the entire world. He in a sense, started from scratch! No one knew too much about him, including me. I remember his speech during the 2004 presidential general election, but I never thought for a moment that he would be the next President of the United States of America. His speech to bring America together has been echoed and re-echoed around the globe.

I had a freshman speech class and a couple of Oral Communication classes. They had little, if any, speaking experience. Well, it was time to go to work. There is always a time (Eccles 3: 1-11). There is a time for everything.

I looked out amongst the speech class. They seemed to be very eager to learn how to speak, because they had signed up for the class. I told them about the San Diego University Speech and Debate tournament. I would like to take some of you; I remember six (6) students were very interested: Kevin McGee, Stanley Sakai, Glen Goodman, Fred Ogimachi, Nancy Romine and Paula Trimble. Glen Goodman did make it to San Diego, but he was killed shortly after in a car accident when he and his sister were on their way to school. She survived, but he did not.

The other five (5) became my pride and joy over the four years I had them in Speech. Indio High School has always been feared throughout the district, and these five (5) students kept the ripples rippling until my call to the ministry in 1975.

These (six) 6 students seemed to have known what category to choose without my telling them. There was only one high school in town, and most students had heard about the speakers, through their older brothers, sisters, or friends or just from reading the newspaper.

Nancy Romine wanted to be in Oratorical Interpretation, a speech already written and published by someone else. Paula Trimble wanted to write an Original Oratory. Stanley Sakai and Fred Ogimachi wanted to debate. Stanley was also in Oratorical Interpretations and Fred was in Extemporaneous Speaking. Glen Goodman wanted to debate, but he had no partner. Kevin McGee decided to debate with him and speak in the Original Oratory. Glen also entered the extemporaneous division.

So, we had two (2) debate teams speaking both affirmatively and negatively in four (4) rounds of competition, two (2) in Original Oratory, two (2) in Oratorical Interpretation, two (2) in extemporaneous speaking. These six (6) students were very knowledgeable and needed little, if any, prompting. Debate material for the school year was available.

They got busy immediately reading and reading and reading!! I even sent these debaters to a law office for more insight on the topic to be debated. Current events, Newsweek, Time magazines and listening to the World news on TV had to be on their minds constantly. Going through the original oratory speeches; picking out attention getting in the first 30 seconds to one (1) minute of the introduction. State the proposition or what you are trying to prove within a minute or two. In the body of the speech, you must prove without a shadow of a doubt by reasoning with sound evidence, such as examples, comparison and contrast, figures, statistics, personal experiences, illustrations and the like . . . In conclusion, state what and why your point is well-taken. Most speeches will have these basics. Now—let's work on delivery, how to stand, when to move, how to gesture, articulation and pronunciation, vocal control to emphasize correctly. This takes plenty of patience to become poised and confident. We worked on these endeavors as we practiced daily. Practice does not make perfect, but it makes for perfection; and the more you practice, the better you will be in the long run.

Being just freshman, these youngsters amazed me when I heard them speak. They sounded like they had been in tournaments before. They did not seem to be novices to me. They were very mature for their age. Some of the students from drama came over every once in a while to see how they were doing. We practiced diligently for about two (2) months. We were going nicely, they thought so too. I would even send them outdoors to the lunch tables and practice every day. They never got tired of practicing, because they knew that the whole purpose of practice was to get better. In the meantime, I had my oral communication classes beginning to learn speeches, because there was a novice tournament coming up at Coachella High School in a couple of months.

The San Diego tournament was coming up. We were confident and ready to go. I always remind the boys and girls how to dress. They always looked good! San Diego, California was about a five hour drive from Indio, but we were on our way in a 12 passenger school van. They were even going over their speeches and the debaters were debating. They really enjoyed what they were doing. They were really having fun! I laugh about that sometimes when I think about how much fun they were having, and today, especially where I live, there is not one tournament that students can go to for fun. I believe they are missing out of an extremely important opportunity. Oh well, life still goes on!

The students were all exuberant after the tournament. Kevin McGee and Paula Trimble won trophies. Glen Goodman and Stanley Salcai were rated excellent in Extemporaneous. The debate teams did not win but one round but gained a tremendous amount of experience. They all did very well, and the fire kept burning as they returned to campus the following Monday morning. The drama students seemed to be enthused and encouraged by how well they did. The upper-class students began to come around more and more. I just thank God; "for He is good and His mercy endureth forever" (Psalm 106:1).

There were other tournaments coming up, and all the speakers could go. The drama department was not rehearsing for another play at this time, so I was fortunate enough to get a chance to hear them speak. I could now understand why they were so feared around the district. They were good!! I was very happy that they came around to me.

King Solomon said it best, "He that handleth a matter wisely shall find good; and whoso trusteth in the Lord, happy is he" (Proverbs 16:20).

I remember the likes of: Joan Peightal, Cary Johnson, Pat Hogue, Wendy Stanley, Claude Dodson, Todd Peterson, David Daniel, Susan Spencer, Cassandra Beavers, Cindy Cotlon, John Bucchino, James Rowe, Nick Zullo, Les Lippitt, Tamara Scott, Nolan Dennett, Janice Hayes, Margaret Romero, Lucy Arrington, Veronica Grey, Brad Hansen, Rosemary Scott, George Klipfell, Dennis Johnson, Janet Matthews, Pam Reagins, Irene Kiaupa, Sandra Weishart, Mike Roberts, Karen Petrie, Albert Huerta, Donato Rodriguez, Mike McFadden, Mary Zapp, Sylvia Aguirre, Janice Low, Sandra Roberts, Jeff Lewis, Beverly Sala, Jan Nordland, Kerry Brooks, Lisa Hadley, Debbie Myers, Cheryl Thomas, Barry Tucker and Barbara VanRamsalaar. I still have the newspaper clipping on most of these students. I do not want to forget Kenny Moreno, T.H. Hinderacker, Ken Knox, John Beyenberg and, of course, my first (six) Stanley Sakai, Fred Ogimachi, Kevin McGee, Glen Goodman, Nancy Romine, and Paula Trimble. There were other names I cannot remember right now, but the names already mentioned were the nucleus of the Speech team. I sure wish I could see them again, maybe not in this life, but in the life to come, (I Corinthians 15:22-23 or I Thessalonians 4:13-18).

I do not want to forget Ray Adams (now deceased), a Black coach, and Bill Snyder were hired the same year I was. They were the two best football coaches to come out of the Coachella Valley. Bill Snyder ended up as football coach at Kansas State University, retired and started coaching again. I saw Bill a few years ago in Kansas City, Missouri at a girl's basketball game; he still looked the same. I was coaching the freshman football team the same time that they coached the varsity. I coached only to find some speakers (smile), and I did find a few. I remember we lost all 6 games that year by just a few points.

At 45 years of age, I was busy as a bee. I was going on Speech tournaments practically every week-end, I was umpiring high school baseball and city league softball games during the afternoons and evenings, I was also the President of the Desert Sands Teacher's Association and a husband and father. All of these responsibilities were w little too much for me, so I backed up a bit.

The Lord was speaking to me, and I started listening, probably for the first time in my life. I became the administrative assistant at the Second Baptist Church in Indio. I read scriptures, prayed, taught Sunday School and spoke once in a while. I enjoyed it, but my Bible Knowledge was way below par. I couldn't find the Book of Amos, let alone telling you what it was all about. I needed to go to a Bible college or somewhere to study more about God's word.

I was having fun going over the Sunday School lesson to one of my Oral Communication classes at school. I did this weekly, and everyone seemed to enjoy it. This gave the students a chance to listen; I would really be preaching sometimes. The students probably had speeches to give themselves, but I believe they were happy when Friday came around. This, at least gave them a little time to relax and forget their speeches until next week.

I did not want to leave Indio. As I look back now, it was because of money. I was at the top of the salary schedule; the money was good, and we as a family did many things together because of money. And the Lord brought to my attention I Timothy 6:10, "For the love of money is the root of all evil, which while some coveted after they have erred from the faith, and pierced themselves through with many sorrows."

That struck a responsive chord, but I wanted to continue teaching while taking evening Biblical studies at a nearby university. I wrote several Bible colleges and seminaries in California for applications. You know what!? That has been over 5 years ago, and I still have not heard from any of them. However, life still goes on!!

Life is like a river, it just goes up and down and around and around; it has so many twists and turns, and no one seems to know its beginning or when it's going to end. Life is a lot like a river, "sometimes up and sometime down, almost level to the ground," some song-writer wrote. If a person does not have faith and trust, he will surely fall when depending on self (Proverbs 3:5).

I knew the Lord was leading me, but I wasn't too sure where. An old Negro hymn says, "Where can I go, where can I go, where can I go but to the Lord?" That's it!! We went to the Lord in prayer!!

SIXTEENTH ANNUAL

University of Nebraska Debate and Discussion Conference

1956

Certificate of Award

of *Superior* quality in *Oratory* is granted

to *Curtis Hayes*

of *Morningside College*

Chairman, Department of Speech

Speakers Win at Redlands High

IHS speakers took first place in sweepstakes at a recent speech tournament to Redlands High School.

At that tournament, 45 points were garnered by 18 Rajah speakers who reached the finals in the Citrus Belt Speech Region affair.

REDLANDS High School was the scene of the event and, according to Mr. Curtis Hayes, IHS Speech instructor, it was a "fantastic display of speaking."

Competition was heavy, as 25 schools were represented by more than 400 participants. With an average of 16 speakers from each school, the Rajahs brought home more than their share of awards, winning ten trophies.

Two of the ten categories were

swept by IHS speakers, meaning that first, second, AND third places were taken in Oratorical Analysis and Oratorical Interpretation.

IHS winners in Oratorical Analysis were Janice Hayes, first place; Donato Rodriguez, second; and Mike McFadden, third.

ORATORICAL Interpretation winners were Margaret Romero, first, and Sylvia Aguirre, second; and Janice Low, third place.

Winners in the Humorous Interpretation category were Cassandra Beavers, first; and Sandra Roberts, third place.

Albert Huerta took a third in Boys' Impromptu and Sandra Weishart rated third in Girls' Extemporaneous.

Finalists (awarded certificates)

were Jeff Lewis, Original Oratory; Beverly Sala and Jan Nordland, Girls' Original Oratory; Kerry Brooks, Girls' Impromptu; Paula Trimble, Oratorical Interpretation; Tammie Scott, Humorous Interpretation; and Debbie Myers and Cheryl Thomas, Girls' Extemporaneous.

MR. HAYES beamed happily after the IHS victory.

"This tournament was a big win for us," he said. "I'm confident we'll go all the way again this year."

The second-place school, Riverside Poly, trailed by 23 points.

Sweepstakes points were tallied on the basis of seven for first place; three for second, two for third and one for each finalist.

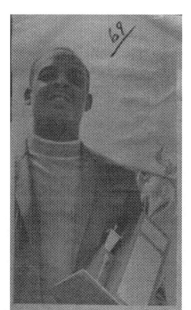

A BIG WINNER — One of the hardest-working and most popular teachers on this campus is Mr. Curtiss Hayes, whose speech students have made him proud by running off with enough trophies, plaques, and certificates this year, to fill a large room. Well done, Mr. Hayes —Kiki Faddick photo

Newspaper clippings
Courtesy of The Desert Sun,
Palm Springs, California

Hayes Is Speakers' Booster

CURTISS HAYES

They were BAD!!

LOADED WITH HONORS — Six of the ten Rajah speech winners who will go on the statewide competition at California State College next month. From the left, Sandy Beavers, Cindy Cotton, John Bucchino, Nick Zullo, Paula Trimble and James Rowe. They rated high in the qualifying events at University of Redlands Saturday.
Staff Photo

Varsity, Novice Teams Both Win Sweepstakes In Contest

2/22/69

Indio High School speech students made a clean sweep of both A and B divisions at the La Verne College Invitational Tournament for high school orators last weekend.

In the A division, the varsity speakers, Nick Zullo and David Daniel led the way in original oratory and oratorical interpretation, respectively, winning first place trophies.

Cindy Cotton took third place

and Rosemary Scott second place in girls' extemporaneous. In boys' extemporaneous, Fred Ogimachi took third place and George Klippel and Dennis Johnston were finalists. John Bucchino was a finalist in dramatic interpretation.

Also participating in the varsity division of the tournament were Glen Goodman, Kevin McGee, Janet Matthews, Lucy Arrington and Irene Kiaupa.

In the novice division, 31 sweepstakes points were amassed.

Winners were Mike Roberts and Sandra Weishart, first and second places, respectively in extemporaneous; James Rowe, second place in dramatic in-

terpretation; Stanley Sakai, third place in original oratory; Paula Trimble, first, Albert Huerta third and Anna Asker finalist in oratorical interpretation. Also taking part were Tammie Scott, Jeff Lewis and Karen Petrie.

"This was a good win," speech coach Curtiss Hayes said. "I have never heard of a school winning two sweepstakes at one tournament before. It was just amazing and unbelievable to have so many students in the finals. The kids really deserved to win."

The Southern District Speech Tournament will be held at Whittier College March 7 and 8.

CHAPTER SEVEN
A CALL TO THE MINISTRY

It was very difficult to leave all of the outstanding speakers at Indio High School and all of our church friends at the Second Baptist Church.

I was growing spiritually at 45 years of age, but I still did not trust God completely. I needed to be strengthened more. Sometimes God allows dire circumstances to come into your life. Our finances were getting low, we had to leave Janice in Los Angeles, we needed a new windshield, I did not know where the Lord was leading me to study his Word, I did not have a job and everything seemed to be quite dark and getting darker in my life. Then, I remembered the Apostle Paul writing to the Church at Corinth, "Be steadfast, unmovable, always abounding in the work of the Lord, forasmuch as ye know that your labor is not in vain in the Lord." (I Cor. 15:58). I needed that assurance, and my faith was strengthened.

I wrote the lady who was renting our house in San Bernardino, that we were coming back to the house and that she had to move. By God's grace and mercy, she moved shortly without any problems. This was another answer to prayer!

We sold our house in Indio without putting up a For Sale sign. This was another indication that we were following the Lord. We sold some of our furniture and gave away the rest. This was another blessing for us, because we helped a lot of people who had little, if any furniture or no money to spend. I know that it is always best to help the less fortunate. Matthew 19:21 says, "Go and sell that thou hast, and give to the poor, and thou shall have treasures in heaven, and come and follow me." What a command!

Our house in San Bernardino looked pretty bad when we arrived. A couple of windows had been shattered and pieces of cardboard were taped to keep out the outside debris from blowing into the house. The hedges around the front lawn seemed to have been untouched for a long period of time. The garage door was leaning so far to one side that it would not completely close. I sighed in dismay and unbelief, thinking how on earth could a house look so unkempt, so untidy, so neglected when people had been living there for seven years?

The back yard was in shambles also. The once pretty oleander shrubs were all disheveled and weeds were growing up the brick walls around the back yard. It was a mess, and I knew that we had a lot of work to do on the house.

Life still goes on!

We went to work on the house, scraping and painting, and mowing and shampooing and trimming hedges and pruning our rose bushes and oleander trees. It was hard work, but we had to do what we had to do. We would sing a lot and took time out to pray while we still worked. In a couple of months, the cute little house at 1173 Trenton Street looked like it did when we rented it seven years before. We were happy; we were elated over a job well done. We put the house up for sale. My faith was being more strengthened now!

I had a long-term substitute teachers' contract at a new junior high school that was just opening. The principal of this new school and I taught at Franklin Junior High at the same time from 1962-66. He was very happy to see me and welcomed me graciously and whole-heartedly. This was another blessing from the Lord. It seems to me now as I look back, the Lord was blessing me and blessing me and blessing me in many ways. All I could say was "Thank You, Lord, praise your name and I Love You!"

One day I met a man, and we began talking about Bible colleges. I told him that I was interested to learn more about God's Word. Without any hesitation on his part, he asked me had I heard about Dallas Theological Seminary in Dallas, Texas. I had not. He went on to say that "if I wanted a good, sound Biblical education that I should contact Dallas seminary." Well, that did not really register, because I did not want to go to any southern state.

I had not heard from any of the Bible colleges that I had written for applications months ago; the house was not selling, but people would come and look, but just looked. My faith was being tried now "real" good, because of God's testings. My faith never wavered, it became stronger.

After about a month, I wrote to Dallas Theological Seminary for an application to study God's Word. Within a few days, I received a 10 page application form. I looked it over a couple of times and put it upon a shelf. I got it down a few days later and went to work filling it out. I had to use scripture to back up my answers, and there were a couple of pages about my personal life; do you smoke? How many do you smoke a day? Do you drink alcohol? How many drinks a day? Have you ever abused women or children? When? Where? Why?

Some of the questions I did not want to answer (smile), but I had to tell the truth about everything and anything. I did not want to be tried and found out that I had lied (Rev. 2:2, Jeremiah 29:8-9).

I was reading the Word of God one day and came across Matthew 10:39. "He that findeth his life shall lose it, and he that loseth his life for my sake shall find it." I did want to serve God, I did want desperately to study His Word, and I did want to give up this world's hang-ups; so I threw away my last package of cigarettes. Now, I could freely and boldly finish the application with optimism and perseverance. I finished it, sealed it and mailed it to Dallas Theological Seminary. I felt good about my honest answers. With God's providential hand at work, I knew that I was going to start in May of 1976. It is around the first of April now and the house had not sold. We wondered, but it was not God's time yet. We changed Realtors which we should have done two months before.

Again, within two weeks, I heard from the seminary. Listen to this: I had been accepted in the Th. M. program; I was given a four year tuition free scholarship and books; free!! That's not all!! There was only one two-bedroom furnished apartment available to scholarship recipients at a very low cost! Wow!! I could not believe it!! Did not God say in Mark 9:23, "If thou canst not believe, all things are possible to him that believeth." I did believe, but it seemed as if the Lord was saying to me, "O ye of little faith", (Matthew 6:30).

My faith was getting stronger and stronger with each day that God allowed my eyes to open. God had already laid out my path to trod, and that was following the trod Jesus took. I had already asked the Lord to guide me in the righteous way of life, according to his power that was working in me (Ephesians 3:20).

The house had not sold yet, but that was OK. I was on my way to Dallas Theological Seminary to study God's Word regardless of whether the house sold or not. Summer school at the seminary would be starting in less than a month.

Another miraculous blessing from God just in the nick of time. God does not come when we want Him to, but He is always on time. Can I get a witness here? I heard an African-American preacher say one day, "You don't hear me!" I heard Dr. Charles Stanley say in one of his sermons, "If you're listening to me, say Amen!"

The Realtor called one morning. He said, "The house is sold!!" The house is sold!! I leaped for joy much like the Ethiopian eunuch did after he was baptized (Acts 9:39). Happy and full of joy was the Samaritan woman who met Jesus at Jacob's well in Sychar (John 4:1-27). She was offered this living water once and for all; she would never thirst again and she would not have to go back to draw water—never in her life!! This is something to shout about!! Hallelujah!! This was worth passing it on to others.

Still rejoicing and praising the Lord, I went to my principal to tell him that I could not finish the school year. He understood, and said, "God be with you, Curtis." The year 1975 was undoubtedly when I unhesitatingly started walking by faith in Jesus Christ and not by sight (2 Corinthians 5:7).

We only had a couple of weeks to sell our furniture. We had a back yard full of picnic tables and lawn chairs. We sold what we could for half the price we could have asked and gave away the rest. We also had two cars we sold very cheap. We packed everything we owned into one car and headed for Dallas, Texas. This was in early May of 1976.

It was raining cats and dogs when we arrived in Dallas. The streets were so flooded that we had to make a couple of detours before we found our upstairs apartment on the corner of Swiss Avenue and Carroll Street. A seminarian who lived downstairs had out keys. We parked in the back and carried our belongings up the back stairs to our two-bedroom furnished apartment. The rooms were very large, and we knew that this was exactly where God wanted us to live. It was within walking distance to the seminary, which made it very nice and convenient.

The next morning we walked down Swiss Avenue to the seminary. We toured the library, bookstore, post office and met some of the faculty and students. There were only five African-Americans at the seminary:

Rev. Eddie Lane was on the staff as a mentor to incoming Black students, Rev Tony Evans was working on his doctorate of theology, Tony Benson, Fred Hendricks, Martin Hawkins and myself were just beginning our Th.M. program. There were students from all over the world, which gave the seminary a cosmopolitan look. I liked that!! White, black, brown, yellow, and red were all represented at the school. To me, it was wonderful to see all these different colors studying God's Word together.

I started my seminary career by taking my first year of Greek in ten weeks. The New Testament is written in the original Greek language, so to interpret the New Testament (Matthew-Revelation) correctly, three (3) years of Greek were required. I took a look at that Greek New Testament and I said, "Oh, my goodness, what on earth are those words, I can't even pronounce them let alone tell you what they mean and what parts of speech they are in the sentences!" I shook my head in dismay, but I knew that the Lord did not bring me this far to leave me. He has promised never to fail me or forsake me (Joshua 1:5).

With that assurance and encouragement, I continued my climb up the rough side of the mountain. We had daily quizzes over vocabulary words. We had to know how they were being used in the scriptures. Were they nouns, adjectives, adverbs, predicate nominatives, direct objects or what? We had to know that to interpret God's Word precisely with understanding. I knew that this course was going to be a hard climb up the hill. I know that anything worth having is not going to be easy.

I failed the first 20 quizzes—twenty (20) straight F's. I was dumbfounded. I was getting discouraged!! The professor was in his thirties, young, and I did not think that he was a very good teacher. He was going so fast in class that I did not know what he was talking about; I even lost interest and again started to quit seminary. I went to the professor for some help, perhaps some tutoring. He was not too interested in my dilemma. I thought he would at least give me some advice or to pray with me or something to help me, but he rather shied me off. That really hurt me to think that a Christian professor would treat me like a nobody, but God always has a ram in the bush (Genesis 22:13). One day I met a seminarian from Nigeria, W. Africa. He had already taken Greek in his country before he came to America. I asked him if he would help me in Greek. He favorably consented that he would. We had a couple of hours practicing day and night. He said now when a word ends in lys, it is a verb, and when a word ends in slo, it is an adverb and on and on he went. The lys and slo are just fictitious letters but Greek word endings have a lot to do with parts of speech. I began to understand the words and how they are used in scripture.

It was not long before I started getting A's on all of my daily quizzes. No one could quite understand how I could make such a drastic change. They did not know that I knew when God sends you, He also equips you. I made it through the first year of Greek OK. I had no problems with second or third year Greek. It came relatively easy for me.

I did not take Hebrew my first year at the seminary. I thought I would wait until my second year, and that is what most of the students did. The first year was tough, too! The professors gave us a lot of work to do, and it took me a long time to finish an assignment, because I did not know how to use all of the necessary tools (books). I burned the candle at both ends many nights.

The Lord never promised that the road would be easy. Storms are inevitable in this life even if you are born again, sanctified and filled with the Holy Ghost. Trials will come to everyone in this life. God will see you through each one.

Curtis Jr. was working in a restaurant shortly after we moved to Dallas. This restaurant was not in the best of neighborhoods. Thugs and drug dealers and pimps and prostitutes roamed Carroll Street, a couple of blocks from the seminary. One night when I picked up Curtis at 11:00 p.m., it was raining hard that night! I saw Curtis running across the street to get into the car. As I was about to pull off, some man came running across the street. I thought he wanted to tell Curtis Jr. something! I rolled down my window about half way and looked over toward my son. I felt something pushing against my neck. This foreigner said, "Give me your money!" I said, "I don't have any money!" He pointed the pistol over toward Curtis and said, "Give me what you've got!" Curtis gave him his last twenty dollar bill. This was a foreigner, because I could tell by his speech. He then said, "I'm sorry I have to do this, but if the white man would give me a job, this would not have been necessary." "Good-night and drive carefully," he said.

I thank God even in this experience! Curtis and I could have been killed that night. Before I picked up Curtis, I had about $400.00 in my billfold that I left at home. Thank God we did have some money at home that this foreigner did not get. Curtis quit that job! What a memoir that was, Wow!! I'll never forget it! Life gets stormy sometimes even when you're facing death, but life still goes on! I just praise His name even in dire situations, for "God is good: for His mercy endureth forever, (Psalm 106:1). Life is a test, to be sure, and if you give up, then you're doomed forever. When anyone tries to be good, evil is always present. My brother-in-law, Bob Motley always says, "That's part of life." Everyone who lives a godly life will suffer persecution (2 Timothy 3:1). James 1:2 says it this way, "Count it all joy when you fall into various temptations."

My first year of taking Hebrew was about to begin. I had another young professor who I did not think was a good teacher at all. He even went faster than the Greek professor had done. Hebrew was a lot worse than Greek! I thought that I would never run into anything as bad as my first semester of Greek. Hebrew caused me to think about dropping out of seminary. Reading those funny looking scribbles (letters) from right to left on a page almost blew my mind sky high. I once again began to lose interest. I could not even learn the Hebrew alphabet, and if you don't know the alphabet, you cannot read anything in Hebrew. I went to class everyday and I did not understand one thing the professor was saying. I was really bewildered and confused at this time in my life.

I heard that this professor gives the same three examinations every year. They were always the same, and they never changed. I went to my next door neighbor who had already taken Hebrew and asked him if I could borrow his exams. He gave them to me; I was really surprised! I looked at those exams and just shook my head. I said to myself, "there is no way—there is no way I can pass; but there was. I became a deceiver, a cheater. I memorized what I could, the rest I wrote down on small wads of paper to put in my pocket. I became a deceiver in seminary, in God's house!! I'm shaking my head now as I write. I did not have to cheat, but I could not think of anything else to do. I did not want to drop out, so I literally cheated my way through first year Hebrew. I just barely knew the alphabet (smile). I was completely dumbfounded.

Passing first year Hebrew with a C-, the second year was about to begin. I knew that I was defeated even before I started. I went to a couple of classes, and I didn't bit more understand anything; it was all Hebrew to me (smile).

I went to my Hebrew professor and laid my cards on the table. I told him quite frankly, but honestly, how I managed to pass. He saw my plight and soon found me a tutor. Praise the Lord! This tutor was also from the country of Nigeria in Western Africa. It was not too long that I began to understand the different words and how they were used in the Old Testament (Genesis-Malachi). It was not too long before I started reading from the right to left with comprehension. I was reading Hebrew from right to left. I was relaxed now, hallelujah, when I went to class. I finally knew everything the professor was saying. I ended up with a B+ average in second year Hebrew. Unbelievable, but true. When God calls you, he equips you!

In my third year of seminary, the Lord blessed us to move into one of the seminary houses on campus. Another blessing had come!! I was working as a yardman at an apartment complex in North Dallas. The complex had a warehouse full of nice furniture that people had left. I went to my manager one day and asked if I could buy some of the furniture. She said, "take what you want." I loaded up my VW camp mobile with black and white furniture two or three times. We decorated our cute two-bedroom house with all black and white furniture. It was very attractive to everyone who visited us. Every now and then, donors would send monetary gifts to the seminary for African-American students. Rev. Eddie Lane would call us to his office to give us a check of $100.00 or $200.00 dollars. What a blessing! God always knows when to send His blessings!

North Dallas was a little too far to go to work, so I looked for something else part-time. I found a part-time elevator position at the Federal Reserve Bank in downtown Dallas. This job gave me a good opportunity to sit down most of the time to study my Greek and Hebrew and other Bible books I had to read. A song-writer wrote, "Count your blessings, name them one by one." I cannot even begin the many blessings that God has bestowed on me. I could not count them all even if I tried.

I had to write a research paper or thesis for my Th.M. degree. I had almost forgotten about it until I ran across it a few days ago. My subject was, "An Analysis to Innovate and Implement a Center of Biblical Studies at Bibleway Bible Church". I did direct this Bible school my last year in seminary. It went well, but I have never heard anything about it since 1980.

Would you believe that a person like me who did not understand Greek or Hebrew would one day say that "I would like to teach Greek or Hebrew at a Bible College when I graduate? I said that, I really said that, but the Lord did not honor my request. Instead He sent me to Liberia, W. Africa as a missionary. I thought about Paul the Apostles' life and how he wanted to go to Jerusalem. Instead, God sent him to Arabia for three (3) years to think about his past life and his Damascus Road experience (Gal 1:17) (Acts 9). Perhaps God was sending me to Africa where I would be alone to reflect on God's goodness and how He brought me out of the world of sin and shame to where I am today because of the Lord, but I do know that Matthew 28:1-9 says, "Go ye therefore and teach all nations, baptizing them in the name of the Father, and of the Son, and of the Holy Ghost." I had no problems with that, but I did not want to go as a missionary. I had always wanted to go to Africa as a teacher, but not a missionary. Sometimes God allows a person to do what they do not want to do for whatever reason. As I look back now, my experience living in Liberia was a blessing. I learned so many things in those four (4) years that I will share with you as I write, "Life Still Goes On!"

I signed up with the Sudan Interior Mission to be a Christian Education Coordinator in Liberia, W. Africa. At the time, I never knew that I had to raise my own support to be a missionary. I was to raise $24,000.00 for a four year stay. Where on earth was I supposed to get that much money? I could have started asking my friends for money, but I have never done that in my life, and I was not going to start that now at fifty (50) years of age. I could have stood on street corners holding up a can for money. I would not have done that either. Someone suggested that I should go to churches for support; that sounded reasonable. The problem with that was I did not know many churches. Let's take them one at a time:

(1) Bibleway Bible Church in Dallas, Texas, pastored by Rev. Eddie B. Lane whose church I attended while in seminary. This church supported me with $50.00 a month for four years.

(2) Oak Cliff Bible Fellowship, Dallas, Texas, pastored by Dr. Tony Evans who was working on his Th. D. when I was in seminary the same time he was. To my recollection, this church took up an offering and said that they would pray for me.

(3) Rev. Rueben Connors pastored a Methodist Church in Dallas, Texas. They took up an offering for me.

(4) Rev. Fred Hendricks, who graduated with me, was pastoring a church in St. Louis, Missouri. They took up an offering for me.

(5) Rev. Tom Smith, who went to pastor a church in Chicago, Illinois before he graduated, took up an offering for me.

(6) Rev. Floyd Brown, pastor of Mt. Zion Baptist Church in Sioux City, Iowa supported me with $50.00 a month for four years. I was ordained as a deacon and licensed to be a minister in this church.

These were the only African-American churches I knew about, and most of them have never supported a missionary. They really did not know what to do. My calling to a foreign field was totally unheard of in the Black church.

My motive was to find the large churches to raise some support. I contacted the First Baptist Church in downtown Dallas, Texas with a membership of over 30,000. I knew this church would at least take up a large sum of money and support me with at least $100.00 monthly. Neither of those happened! I became dissolutioned at this point!!

Then I remembered the Apostle Paul writing to the church in Philippi, Philippians 4:6-7, "Be anxious for nothing but in everything by prayer and supplication with thanksgiving, let your requests be made known to God. And the peace of God, which passeth all understanding, shall keep your hearts and minds through Jesus Christ."

Those words pepped me up a bit. I graduated with a young man who went to pastor a small church in Dell City, Oklahoma. Rev. Gerald Fonte and I were close friends in seminary. He was tickled pink when I contacted him about speaking in the church to raise support for me on foreign soil. He was very excited about it. I remember driving through the city looking for the street where the church was located. Driving slowly down the main street in this small city, we noticed the people looking and no doubt wondering where on earth we were going. I do not know for sure, but I do not think that there were any African-Americans living in this country town. We finally found the store-front church. Again, I shook my head in disbelief. We entered the church to find no pews, but only a couple of benches and a few folding chairs and about ten people in attendance. We gave our presentation. The people were enthralled and fascinated; a captivating audience to our surprise! They took up $1,500.00 that evening and this little church supported us with $50.00 a month for four years. I truly learned a lesson from this experience while traveling the deputation trail. It is not the "big" church or is it people with money that will support you. Your support will come from widows and the small mission minded churches. Well, what an eye opener that was and it was just what I needed. The Lord got my attention by letting me know to just tell the people where you're going, why you are going and what you will be doing in W. Africa. That made a lot of sense to me. Orientation for missionary candidates would be held in Cedar Grove, New Jersey in a few weeks. We went back to Dallas to say good-bye to our church family and to our friends. This time around, we left all of our beautiful black and white furniture to whosoever needed a furnished two-bedroom house on the campus at Dallas Theological Seminary. Another blessing to help somebody!

Curtis Jr. had gotten married by this time, so he would not be going to Africa with us. Collin was about fourteen (14) years of age, so he had no other choice. He definitely, however, did not want to go to Africa. School was just about to begin in Liberia, and one thing that prompted Collin in not wanting to go was he did not want to be late for the beginning of school. Our support was gradually coming in but not fast enough for us to leave in time for school.

There was a missionary there who was on her way to Abijan, a French speaking country in Ivory Coast where most of the missionary kids went to school. With enough support for Collin to go, this missionary lady obliged to take Collin with her to Abijan. What a blessing!! Collin was blessed to start his freshman year in time, and we had a place to stay in Cedar Grove, New Jersey while raising the rest of our support. It was difficult to see Collin leave us, but God always knows best. He is omniscient (all knowing)!!

CHAPTER EIGHT
IN PREPARATION FOR LIBERIA

We were still short of the $24,000 needed to go to Liberia, so we had to stay in New Jersey a little longer than we planned.

All prospective new missionary candidates had to meet for a two-week orientation briefing. There were about forty (40) of us, and they were very nice to us. They would be going to different parts of the world to minister. Everybody was real excited! We were too!!

One Sunday we visited a Black church in E. Orange, New Jersey. I do not remember this pastor's name or the church. I do remember, however, that this church was very mission-minded and supported us with $50.00 a month for the next four (4) years. This gave us a lot of hope to think that this church would support us and did not know one thing about us. They believed in helping someone who was helping themselves to help others! The blessings just kept on coming in!! They never stop when you put your trust in the Lord. He always makes a way out of no way!! He always makes what seems to be impossible-possible!! What an awesome God we serve!

I learned that Liberia was colonized by freed American slaves in 1820, and the Republic of Liberia became independent in 1847. The freed slaves called themselves Americo-Liberians which became a big problem in the country for the next 150 to 200 years. The freed slaves were somewhat educated, dressed nicely, spoke English and had a little money. The indigenous Liberians were less educated, dressed in their native garb, spoke very little English and had very little or no money.

Liberia has a population of 3.5 million people who represent about sixteen different ethnic groups speaking sixteen different dialects. Situated on approximately 43,000 square miles, the country of Liberia is well-watered on the coast of West Africa. It has never been bothered with tornadoes, hurricanes, droughts or such things, but it does have a history of turmoil between the freed Negro slaves who called themselves Americo-Liberians and the natives who had been there long before the freed slaves went there.

After the American Revolutionary War, the slaves were promised their freedom if they sided with the British. Many did and left America for Sierra Leone in West Africa. Unfortunately, many of them died of malaria and yellow fever.

It was a subtle move in the first place by prominent American leaders, such as, Henry Clay, Francis Scott Key, Benjamin Franklin and Daniel Webster. Even Thomas Jefferson said, "They had to go!" In July 26, 1847, the country was born! The freed slaves left America for Africa.

Americo-Liberians to some degree took over the government and the indigenous natives were not allowed to participate in the legislature until years later. Hence, animosity continued to brew for many years to come. The Americo-Liberians tried to live in Liberia and America at the same time, but that does not work. A saying goes, "if you're going to live in Liberia, then be a Liberian; if you still want to be American, you should not have left."

Liberia is a country of rolling hills that stretches for miles and miles without seeing much of anything. That statement reminds me of driving from Roswell, New Mexico to Albuquerque, New Mexico. There is nothing to see but a few cattle from time to time (smile).

The Liberian flag resembles the American flag; the only difference is the number of stars and stripes in red, white and blue. The Liberian motto is "The love of Liberia brought us here."

Our departure was delayed a few more weeks because of a coup d'état, a decisive move on the part of Sgt. Samuel Doe, a military strategist, who took over the government and became the president. Thousands of lives were lost and many people had to flee to neighboring countries. The country was at war again!! The former president, William Tolbert had just been assassinated.

"Shall we go or shall we not," I thought. God says, "Go!" After reading about all of the problems that Liberia was still having, I was ready to go!! I was not fearful in the least, because I knew that God would take care of me, living or dead.

Our son, Collin had been gone about a month now when my wife and I boarded a Pan-Am 747 in New York City. A bomb threat scattered all of us off the plane back into the airport until the plane was searched. Nothing was found, however, so back on the plane we went. We flew through two nights of peace and happiness and quietness. What a flight! It was awesome, it was breathtaking; it was an assurance that God keeps his promises!

Looking out the window from the airplane as we were getting ready to land at Robert's Field in Paynesville, Liberia, I could see the tall coconut and palm trees borderlining the Atlantic Ocean. I could see the shanties (huts) off in the distance and people walking to and fro carrying vegetables, fruit, fish or whatever. The runway is so close to the ocean that I thought we were going to crash. That was a frightening moment to be sure. You brought us this far Lord, to crash? (smile)

Entering the airport, we saw several soldiers carrying carbines and M-1 rifles. Some soldier stopped me to ask me, "Where I was going?" I said, "To the warehouse to pick up my boxes." At this time two or three young boys came up wanting to carry our bags and show us where the warehouse was. We had previously sent about twenty boxes of paper, envelopes, toilet paper, soap, deodorant, toothpaste, toothbrushes, pencils, ink pens, shaving lotion, Vaseline, stamps, cameras, radios and much more. We went to the warehouse to pick them up. Would you believe that only two boxes were there, and they had been opened and picked over? What a welcome this was to Liberia! We picked up our two boxes!!

Liberia has two seasons: a rainy season from late April to late September and a dry season from October to April. It was now in the middle of September and the rains were here.

We were picked up by a missionary who took us to the missionary compound to the guest house. I remember all the potholes we had to dodge as we drove to the compound ELWA, which stands for Eternal Love Winning Africa. This was a radio station that broadcasted to several countries in Western Africa. We would stay in the guest house until our house was ready.

The Atlantic Ocean was only about 50 yards away from the guest house. Sometimes it would rain for 10 to 12 hours without stopping, let up a minute or two and rain steadily for another 10 to 12 hours. I had never seen it rain like that in my life. With all the rain and the waves coming in from the ocean, it was very difficult to sleep. The time change did not make it any easier. After a week or so of this devastating experience, the director of the mission informed us that we would not be moving into the house at ELWA. The house was being saved for missionaries who had been delayed somewhere.

Oh well, life still goes on!!

We moved into a two-bedroom upstairs apartment in Sinkor, Liberia, about 10 miles from ELWA. Actually, this might seem a little sad to you who are reading this memoir, but on the contrary. This was another blessing from God. We did not want to live by the ocean anyway where most of the missionaries were living. There was a hospital on the compound but just a handful of Liberians. We wanted to live in the midst of them; we wanted to live around Liberians, to become like Liberians.

The Lord blessed in His usual mighty way. Sinkor was a city of 10,000 situated about 5 miles from downtown Monrovia, the capital city. There was a small church behind our apartment where 50 to 60 young people came every Sunday to worship. This church was pastored by different missionaries from time to time. These young people could speak a dialect, but most of them could speak some English. It took quite a while for me to get use to their pigeon English (esus J ofs way oo way oo too) Jesus love you too! I learned how to speak pigeon English, and that really made my stay enjoyable. I did not try to learn any of the sixteen dialects spoken in the country. Greek and Hebrew in seminary were enough languages for me (smile).

These young people would bring their wash boards and other handmade instruments to church and play until their hearts were contented. They would rejoice, sing and shout for a whole hour or more. They would also give testimonies about how good God has been to them. The would literally cry when testifying. They never complained and most of them had absolutely nothing. They just praised God to be alive; it was really something to behold! Many of their brothers and sisters and even their parents were killed by soldiers when Sgt. Doe took over the government. I have never seen people who were so happy when most of them didn't know if they were going to have another meal or not. They lived from day to day. Wow!! What more could I have learned from these young boys and girls? I stand in awe sometimes today looking hind-sight to their faith and trust they had in Jesus Christ. What a blessing this had been to me, and by the way, it still is.

If they can live this kind of existence for 10, 20 or 30 years, I can certainly do it for the next 3 years until my furlough was due.

Two missionary ladies lived in an apartment adjacent to us upstairs. They were very nice and helped us adapt to Liberian customs and culture. They also went to the same church behind our apartment. From time to time after church they would have all the young people stay for dinner.

Jollof rice was the main meal on Sundays. It was rice, of course mixed with chicken, beef meat, fish, and sometimes pork meat poured over with palm butter or palm oil. It was very tasty! It was placed in a big bowl on the floor around which 15 or 20 people sat. After prayer; they always prayed before they ate. I remember this one boy praying . . . Wow!! He even cried when he prayed because he was so happy!! I was waiting for the spoons, knives and forks to come around, but they never did. I noticed the hands going down into the bowl and the food was scooped up into their mouths out of their hands. I said, "No way am I going to do that!" When you are in Liberia, you do what the Liberians do. So, I dug in with my hands and ate.

They were very happy to see that I wanted to be one of them, and that's what it's all about. That is what it is all about. After that day, I had no more problems eating with my hands with other people's hands in one dish eating Jollof Rice. What a turnabout! What a change in my life; unbelievable, but true.

The rainy season was still in progress. I remember hearing drums coming from a neighboring village early every morning. Young people especially would celebrate by dancing in the rain. Some children from 2 years of age to perhaps 14 or 15 would dance up and down the street in front of the apartment naked. I could not believe my eyes! I mean naked as a jailbird, boys and girls. They were thankful that God had sent rain so their crops of rice, barley, corn, potatoes, greens, cassava and whatever else they planed would soon be ready to harvest. Psalm 100: 1-5 says, "Make a joyful noise unto the Lord", and they really did. They were not ashamed to glorify God by this exercise, but this was their culture; this was their culture; something they have done for years in Liberia. If I had been a little younger, I might have gone dancing up the street with them (smile).

One day a man came by the apartment begging for money and food. I let him talk. He went on and on telling me that his wife was pregnant with nothing to eat at home. He also had two small children who were hungry and had not eaten in days. He talked and talked until he started crying "real" tears. I mean he really put on a good show. I did not know whether to believe him or not. I put some non-perishable food in a sack, and said, "le go ó." That's means let's go. I wanted to go home with him to see if he was telling me the truth. I had already been informed about how the Liberians could lie. I gave him the sack to carry. He lived about 3 miles and we started walking. As we got closer to his house, he started walking faster. He lived up a high hill behind large boulders, and he started to run. There was no way that I could keep up, because the big rocks were too big for me to jump over, and all the little huts looked the same. I saw him jumping over the huge rocks, darting in between the huts that I finally lost sight of him. I walked back down the hill to the main road, caught me a taxi and went home. I told myself that, "if I ever see him again, I'm going to beat him." Would you believe I saw him again about two years later? I played like I did not recognize him, but I did!

Life still goes on!!

Sinkor was a nice place to live. We lived across the street from a small village of about 200 people, and from my upstairs balcony, I could see the women coming to draw their daily water from a well and carrying the bucket(s) back to their one room shacks. This was just another one of my experiences that I will never forget. Most of the people were very nice and helpful in many ways. It was time for us to move again, and we would surely miss all of the young people at the church behind where we lived. From Sinkor to Paynesville: Life still goes on!

CHAPTER NINE
FROM SINKOR TO PAYNESVILLE

This was another blessing from the Lord! Paynesville was only 3 miles from ELWA, a city of about 1,000 people with several churches in which to minister. We would be moving into a very cute two-bedroom furnished stucco house. It even had a bathroom with a stool, tub and a shower. What a blessing this was!

We did have two big barrels outside to catch water for dire circumstances which were many. Liberia is known for its water shortage especially during the dry season. Generators were sometimes broken down and no water could come into the city. With the barrels outside, we used the water to flush the toilet (smile).

I was told that this house was owned by some wealthy people from Freetown, Guinea. When the coup d'état came and the soldiers were roaming the villages killing up everybody, the owners left the house evidently in a hurry and fled eastward. Thousands of people fled to neighboring countries at this time. It was a very sad time for many of the people. Paynesville had also been ransacked as were other cities in and around Monrovia. It reminded me when I first saw Seoul, South Korea thirty years before.

The Lord blessed us with a 1976 Honda Civic at a relatively cheap price. There were not too many automobiles in Liberia, only the president and staff had them. We were considered to be rich by many because we had a car.

I lived about two blocks from a gravel road in Paynesville and during the rainy season, I could not drive down the muddy road to our house.

I remember taking off my shoes and socks, rolling up my pant legs and walking the necessary distance home. I thank God that I was able to do that! There are literally thousands of Liberians who do not live near a gravel road and have to walk down muddy paths for miles to get to their huts. I have seen it with my own eyes. I have walked down those muddy roads to minister God's Word. The Liberians were happy as a lark, singing, "Precious Lord, take my hand, lead me on, let me stand. I am tired, I am weak, I am worn. Through the storm, through the night, lead me on to the light, take my hand, precious Lord, and lead me home." These songs and others were brought to Liberia by the freed slaves. They could really sing as they walked down and up the muddy roads.

I remember on one occasion, I had to drive about 150 miles to a small village to preach. The chief of this small village had three (3) wives. He would stay with each wife one week at a time. I had heard of men in some countries who had more than one wife, but this was the first time I had actually seen it with my own eyes. One wife was in her upper teens, another one in her middle or late 20's and a third one in her middle or late 40's. They all cooked and ate together as one big happy family. Of course, in Liberia, this was ok as long as the man could take care of them. I still shake my head in remembrance of that lifestyle. What a memoir!!

The rainy season had stopped and the dry season had arrived. I was fortunate to see the coal and charcoal mines off in the distance in Bombi Hills, Liberia, and I visited firsthand the Firestone Rubber Plantation. It was very gigantic with thousands of rubber trees as far as the eye could see. The workers would speedily go from tree to tree, cutting the bark and catching the sap in buckets to be taken to a big container truck! I could have watched this all day, but I had to go and preach.

It was very hot and humid this day in church where I had three (3) different interpreters. The people had paper to drive away the mosquitoes and flies. It was awful, but life still goes on!

It was time for dinner. I saw this red looking beef meat, snake meat, and Lord knows what else to be poured over rice. There was also a dish called Fufu, a gummy substance of whatever. I took a spoon full of this Fufu and chewed and chewed but could not swallow it. I excused myself and told everyone that I had to go study for my next sermon.

I walked though the village only to find an old woman who was selling bread and warm soda water. This is what I ate (smile). Life still goes on! I was happy to leave that part of Liberia to Paynesville knowing that I had something decent to eat when I got home.

I was learning a lot about Liberia by this time, and it was a very difficult place to live, but I knew the road would not be easy. The Lord sent me here, and I was going to make the best of whatever situation I faced.

I was blessed to be around several churches where I could minister. There was a very large church on the ELWA compound where I preached for six months or more. People who live in Liberia were from all over the world, and the church at ELWA was mixed with all these different colors of people. It was really a good mixture of people represented in this part of the world. It was a delight, privilege, and a wonderful opportunity to preach to these massive audiences. I cherish it deeply!

I taught a couple of Bible classes at the Carver Bible Institute in Paynesville, and I also taught theology at the Liberian Baptist Theological Seminary, also in Paynesville. On my way to these two institutions of higher learning, I would sometimes pick up four or five children walking down the road to their elementary school. They were very happy I picked them up, and I was happy myself seeing these Liberian children continuing their education. I was blessed!!

I would go out to the mission compound once in a while just to be alone. I wrote my best sermons sitting near the ocean under coconut or palm trees. These trees are very high, some reaching a height of 60 to 80 feet. I remember one day I saw several young boys climbing up those trees. They were hard to climb, because there isn't anything to hold while climbing. They would bring me some coconuts to take home. I would give them about fifty (50) cents.

There was also a dancing group that practiced dancing near the beach almost every day. Those drummers could really play those drums and could those dancers dance; they could really "shake it up"!! I enjoyed them immensely. I am shaking my head now to see these young people who could synchronize such togetherness without missing a beat. This was the best dancing group I have ever seen. I can hear those drums now. I asked one of the drummers one day why he beat those drums the way he did. He simply said, "I'm trying to beat the devil and his demons out of Liberia!! The military had just taken over the government at this time, and what he said could have been a wise word from a drummer's mouth.

I remember driving around the city one day, and it was a pitiful sight. Most of the buildings and houses were unoccupied, the streets were littered with all kinds of debris, and I cannot explain what the Hotel Africa looked like. We stayed there one night and there was no running water or anything. Most of the windows had been broken out and the bathrooms were all out of order. People had to go behind buildings, houses or wherever to go to the bathroom. It was awful, but by God's grace, I made it. Thank God, I made it. There was no Burger King or McDonald's or Kentucky Fried Chicken to get something to eat. I remember telling myself that when I got back to America the first thing I'm going to do is to find a McDonald's and get a Big Mac, large fries and a medium Dr. Pepper with ice. Would you believe that was exactly what I did when I reached New York City!!? That was another blessing God allowed me to do!

I went out to the mission compound one day to buy some gas and a few missionaries were laughing and talking about something exciting!! To my surprise, they told me that chickens, potatoes and polish sausage had just arrived and had them at a store in downtown Monrovia.

I drove an ELWA car that day, and it was probably a good thing that I did. I had absolutely no idea at all that I was going to run into any trouble. The soldiers were standing all around downtown, and especially near the store. Beggars were plentiful!

My wife and I shopped that evening, and we were surprised that the store was stocked with meat and fruits, and everything looked good and fresh. We spent about $200.00 and were very happy that we had that much money to spend. We bought about a dozen of chickens, three 10 lb bags of potatoes, plenty of hamburger and bacon and hotdogs and sausage. We really stocked up good, loaded the groceries in the trunk of the car with the help of several small boys helping us and off we went home. It was about 6:15 pm. We passed by the Executive Mansion where the new president, Sgt. Samuel Doe was staying. Would you believe that within seconds, our car was stopped and surrounded by hundreds of soldiers?

"Get out, they yelled; Get out!" We had no idea what was happening! "Get out!! Get out, they yelled!!" A soldier opened the car and pointed an M-1 rifle to my head and told me to pump. He said, "Pump!" I said, "I don't know what you're talking about." He demonstrated it to me by stretching his arms out and bending his knees up and down, up and down, up and down. About that time, several of Sgt. Doe's assistance came and saw ELWA, Eternal Love Winning Africa on the sides of the car and stopped the would have been melee. They told us that no cars could pass by the Executive Mansion after 6:00 pm in the evening. We didn't know anything about that; no one had ever told us. They searched our car, took a few Bibles which were in the back seat. We showed them our identification cards as missionaries at ELWA. They let us go but reminded us not to pass this way after 6:00 pm in the evening. We said, "OK and thanked them." What a scary moment that was! What a memoir!!

We went back to the missionary compound and told a couple of missionaries about our life-threatening time with some soldiers. I found out later that this one soldier in particular wanted me to pump, go up and down until I fell completely out. I said to myself, "If I ever see that soldier again, he had better run for his life." Would you believe that I saw that same soldier a couple of years later walking downtown without his uniform or his rifle? I said to my wife, there he is, there he is!! I stopped the car and started to go after him, but my wife said, "let him go!"

Life still goes on!

We took home plenty of food to last us a couple of months. We were happy!! We had been in Liberia about three (3) months at this time, and we had not had any fried chicken. I laugh about that now, but it wasn't funny then, just something we had to do without.

A few days later, our electricity went off. It always does for an hour or two. This time, however, we had no power for four days. We took most of our meat to the mission complex and left all our meat with another missionary. Generators were always working at ELWA!

I went back and forth daily to get something to cook. It was only about 3 miles from where we lived, so that was no big problem. We never knew when our electricity would come on or go off. This was nearly a four-year occurrence of how we had to live. We praised the Lord even during these times.

Collin came home for the Christmas break. It was good to see him after four (4) months. He looked good, had grown some and he could speak French! He liked Abidjan and the school he was attending. We were thankful for that. He met a few friends in Liberia the few weeks he was there. They played basketball or soccer just about every day. We went to the church in Sinkor, and all the young people fell in love with Collin. It was a warm welcome to Liberia for him. He enjoyed the people, the church and the Jollof rice. Saying good-bye to Collin this time wasn't as bad as it was in New Jersey the first time he left. He was a junior now in high school, and he would spend his last year in Liberia.

Looking back 2-1/2 years when the Lord sent me to Liberia, I thank the Lord everyday for how He has made me a better person because of living in Liberia. When I first went to Liberia, I was somewhat proud, somewhat arrogant, somewhat self-centered, somewhat suspicious and somewhat unlovable. God spoke to my heart, "Love one another as I have loved you; (John 13:34). With that admonition my whole attitude began to change about the people God sent me to minister. Sometimes God puts you in situations for your sake, for you to grow up spiritually and trust the Lord more. What a re-awakening thought!!

I started loving these Liberians like they were my very own; and in a sense, they were. We are our brother's keeper!! One thing about Liberia I learned from the beginning was their extended family relationship. I have witnessed extended families, such as mother, father, son-in-laws, daughters-in-law, grandchildren, uncles, aunt, nieces, nephews, cousins and on and on, living together on straw mats on the floor. Extended families stick together like super glue sticks. This is one of the strengths that have helped Liberia to stick together and to pray together. Those extended family members who worked took care of those who did not work but stayed home, cleaned house, cooked and planted small gardens and/or sold dried fish, charcoal, onions and cassava in front of their homes. The Liberians do know how to help one another. This needs to be learned and practiced in the United States of America.

I have never met so many nice and friendly people as I did in Liberia in a long, long time. I praise the Lord for getting me out of myself long enough for me to love the unfortunate, the illiterate, the uneducated and the poor. They taught me more about spiritual things than I taught them. They know the power of the Holy Spirit and how to be controlled by Him! It is a good thing to be saved, sanctified and filled with the Holy Spirit but anyone who has those characteristics must be controlled by Him, like a drunk man is controlled by his liquor. Praise the Lord for the Holy Spirit!!

Sometimes our full support never came through every month, and we had to live by faith from day to day. The Liberians, 9 out of 10 of them have to live this way 40, 50, or 60 years of their lives. Now, if they can live this way for all of these years, then we can too for only a mere four years. I claim Liberia's motto: "The love of Liberia brought me here."

In 1982, my mother in the States had a massive stroke, and she suddenly went home to be with the Lord. I flew home to Sioux City,

Iowa to be with family and friends during this time. My mother looked beautiful as she previously looked at 39 years of age. She never passed that age, but now she was 72. The funeral was at the Mt. Zion Baptist Church, eulogized by Pastor Floyd E. Brown.

I stayed with my dad a few weeks to make sure he would be ok. I flew back to New York only to get a telephone call from my sister, Pearline, who told me that dad had pneumonia and was in a hospital. I did not return to Sioux City thinking that my father would soon be released. He was but he too went to be with the Lord six months later.

I had already flown back to Liberia and my meager budget would not allow me to go back. I thank God that I did have the time to spend with him before I left.

Back in Liberia, I still saw the soldiers walking up and down the street with their loaded carbines and M-1 rifles. I will always claim 2 Timothy 1:7, "For God hath not given us the spirit of fear, but of power and of love and a sound mind." I was never afraid in Liberia. Hallelujah!!

The more I write the more I think about how God protected me, particularly in Liberia. I remember taking pictures of the University of Liberia and other buildings and people on the street when some soldier came by and snatched the camera out of my hand. He said, "No one takes pictures here!" He took my camera with him. Life still goes on!

The year was 1983, and Collin had finished his junior year in Abijan, Ivory Coast in West Africa. He would spend his senior year at a preparatory high school in Sinkor, Liberia. He was on the varsity basketball and played well. He graduated with high academic honors, and he could really speak French now.

It was time for us to go back to America and raise support to return to Liberia in 1985. It was very difficult to leave Liberia, just like it was to leave Indio High School in 1975 and Franklin Junior High School in 1966. It was now 1984.

I would miss all of my church friends. I would miss my walks along the Atlantic Ocean watching the small boats come to shore loaded with fish. I would miss the hundreds of taxicabs jammed with passengers headed toward waterside, an area near the river to buy foodstuffs. I would miss the music and the dancing and the beating of drums early in the morning. I would not miss the rainy or the dry seasons (smile). I would not miss all of the soldiers either. I would miss all of the beggars in front of the stores. I felt really sorry for them, and I tried to help monetarily when I went shopping.

I would like to go back to Liberia someday. I understand now as I write that Liberia is on the move to unify all of the people. Thank God for the new president who is determined to bring this to its fulfillment! I praise God for her perseverance and her love for all the people in Liberia.

President Ellen Johnson Sirleaf said on page 334 of her book, "This Child Will be Great, we are moving forward. Our best days are coming. The future belongs to us because we have taken charge of it. Our people are already building our roads, cleaning up our environment, creating jobs, rebuilding schools, bringing back water and electricity. We are making Liberia home once again. We are a good people, we are a kind people. We are a forgiving people—and a God-fearing people. So, let us begin anew, moving forward into a future that is filled with hope and promise. We cannot fail!"

Excerpt from *This Child Will be Great.*

CHAPTER TEN
TO AMSTERDAM, PARIS AND DALLAS

We flew on KLM to Amsterdam in the Netherlands. Amsterdam was one of the most beautiful cities I had ever seen. Everything was so plush and green. The buildings looked as if they were just built when they had been built years ago. The city was clean as a whistle as the saying goes. The streets were not littered up with debris or anything of its kind. The small boats were really delightful especially at night as they would go up and down the river as they toured visitors.

I noticed the couple of days that I was there that most of the people were smoking cigarettes and some were outright smoking "Pot". I had never seen anything like this in my life.

We toured the Art galleries, the museums and other marble looking buildings. Our tour guides were all smoking as they walked throughout the building showing us different things. It was awesome! Unbelievable but true.

Our hotel was spotless and the food was very tasty. All of our waiters and waitresses were smoking while they worked. There was a large train station in Amsterdam where thousands of people go to catch a train to other European countries. While waiting for their train to come, people would sit on the grass outside to listen to some jazz or to whatever or whoever was in the city at that time. I remember listening to an African American playing a tenor saxophone. He really had the crowd on their feet. It was very enjoyable. I would also like to visit Amsterdam again, a very beautiful city where everyone smoked. I ate something while I was there that really upset my stomach.

We flew to Paris, France after spending a couple of days in the Netherlands. Paris is also a very beautiful city but not as beautiful as Amsterdam. The people in Amsterdam were very cordial and friendly, but not in Paris. I had a stomach virus or something while I was in Paris, so I didn't enjoy myself in that city. The people were rather unfriendly and if you did not know how to speak French, you were in real trouble. Fortunately, Collin could speak French, so the people could not fool him and put him on the wrong subway. He and his mother had a wonderful time touring Paris by subway trains. I stayed in my room for two days. From my upstairs window, I could see the majestic Eiffel Tower glittering in the distance. I never realized that it was so gigantic. It was a sight to behold, to be sure. I also noticed some Black boys doing a dance called the "breakdown!" I had never seen that before. In Liberia, I did not have a TV, so I did not know what was going on anywhere (smile). Those were the only things I saw in Paris worth mentioning.

We boarded a plane in Paris for New York City. After the long flight, I thought we were going to crash in the bay. The runway at LaGuardia Airport was too close for comfort as we landed. I went to a doctor the next day to get rid of my dissipated virus. After a shot and a few pills, I got OK. We flew to Dallas, Texas where we would spend the next year while raising more support. I was very fortunate to get a one year contract teaching a couple of classes at Dallas Bible College as a missionary on leave. It went well, but the support was slow in coming. It was so slow that we decided, perhaps, the Lord did not want us to go back to Liberia. To be honest, we really did not want to go back. We thought that doing deputation all over again was just a little too much for us at that time. Liberia was a wonderful learning experience. We had already gone when the Lord said "Go!" We went and our tenure was up, so why go back? We felt good about our decision.

I then began looking for a full-time teaching position. I found one in a prestigious, elite high school south of downtown Dallas. I was hired to teach Speech the day I was interviewed.

This high school was only for the professional minded students. They were screened very carefully before being accepted. I liked that!! They had to dress like professionals; no jeans or tennis shoes could be worn. I liked that also.

My classroom was like a college lecture hall with desks up and coming down row by row to the podium at the bottom of the steps. I had to look up and around to teach the more than 50 students who were a mixture of freshman, sophomores, juniors and seniors. This was a nice mixture of people just like the church at ELWA in Liberia. There were students from all around the world. Whites, Blacks, Browns, Yellows and Reds made up the class. It was awesome!!

The first day of class I spent going through the syllabus telling the students what was required for the course and my expectations. Some Black boy, nice looking, dressed neatly came in late and walked slowly all the way down the steps and slid into a seat on the first row. Some students giggled a bit, but I didn't. I continued with my course outline. This boy kept doing the same thing for a few more days. I kept him after class one day and reminded him of his tardiness and walking slowly down the steps and sliding into his seat to get some attention from his peers. He told me that he would not be tardy again. He did OK for about a week, then back to his old habit. I had enough of his foolishness. One day he was coming in late, and I said with a loud voice, "Get out of here, go to the principal's office and don't come back here until I see your parents!" I went to see the principal after class and told him what this boy was doing. The principal said, "You know, Mr. Hayes, you are the only teacher who has stood up against this boy, I'll notify his parents!" The kid was a senior who had gotten away with mischievous deeds for three years. It was time for him to stop acting like a child. It was time for him to stop!

Two weeks later his mother came prancing down the hall when I met her. She said, "You must be Mr. Hayes, my boy wants out of your class, you are mean and cruel to him, you're always blaming him for being tardy and on and on she went". I said, "Sit down lady, your son is the most obnoxious student I have ever had. I want him to stay in my class." He stayed in my class and became one of the best students I ever had during my 25 years of teaching. Proverbs 22:6 says, "Train up a child in the way he should go, and when he is old, he will not depart from it." This is what I have always tried to do. Dr. Russell Eidsmoe used to tell all of his in-coming teachers, "Don't let any student get away with any wrong doings." I have never forgotten those words, never!! Of all the thousands of students that I had the privilege to teach, I only had to reprimand three (3) students: one at Woodrow Wilson Junior High School, one at Highland Junior High School, and one at South Dallas

High School. That's really not a bad track record! I thank God that He gave me a love for students the first day I taught in 1956. Praise God!

What a wonderful journey that has been. I taught at this South Dallas High School for another couple of years with no additional problems.

At this time in my life (1986-1987), God began speaking to me in that still small voice. He seemed to be saying, "Curtis, you have been faithful over a few things, now I'm going to make you ruler of many things." (Matthew 25:23).

I was attending St. Luke United Methodist Church during this time. Dr. Zan Holmes was the pastor of this very large church. He had been in the Texas Legislature for a number of years in the 1970's. He was now a theology professor at Perkins School of Theology at Southern Methodist University in North Dallas. I could not believe that this African American church was so spiritual, and the people were so nice and friendly. This church was more Pentecostal than United Methodist. I attended several weeks to make up my mind as to what kind of church that worshipped like this. Dr. Zan Holmes could really preach and sing too! The 100 member choir could really "shake it up". It had several soloists who had melodious voices, and the choir would rock to the music while clapping their hands. I loved it!! I loved it!!

One Sunday my wife and I went forward to join the church. He said, "I have been seeing you two for a few weeks sitting in the back. I'm glad you came down today. Sitting in his office after church that Sunday morning, I told my story. He was somewhat impressed; I suppose, and invited me to join him in the pulpit every Sunday morning and evening. He had about eight (8) assistants, and all of us had to meet once a week to find out what we were supposed to do in the worship services.

I became part of the whole and I was loving it. I sometimes opened up the services in prayer, reading Scripture, and once in a while would preach in the evening services.

One day Pastor Holmes asked me if I was ready to pastor a church. I said, "No—not yet". Another month or two went by and he asked me again if I was ready to pastor. I said again, "No—not yet." He asked me the same question a month or two later. This time I said, "I'm ready!" "I'm ready to go!"

CHAPTER ELEVEN
FROM MISSIONARY TO PASTOR!

When I graduated from seminary in 1980, I told the Lord that I did not want to be a missionary and I did not want to pastor a church. Would you believe that from 1980-1984, I was a missionary in Liberia, W. Africa? Now, I'm on my way to be a pastor in the United Methodist Church. What I did not want to do was what I ended up doing. I am now substituting in the Roswell Independent School District, something I did not want to do either. These seemingly untrue statements have become true in my life.

Life still goes on!! I'm packing up again; this time to Lubbock, Texas. We found our nice little two-bedroom house nearly all furnished next door to the church. The church was very nice on the outside and inside. They had taken care of it. The lawn was neatly mowed, and the flowers in front of the church were very pretty. The former pastor was there moving out some of his last belongings. He showed me the different rooms for classes and the sanctuary was very beautiful and red carpet was throughout the church. It was really a nice looking church and I was very happy to be the pastor.

The membership was around 70 people, mostly African Americans who lived on the Eastside of Lubbock. We did have one Chinese member and one Anglo young man both of whom attended Texas Tech University. I would say that this was the most elite group of people in Lubbock. Most of the members were very well educated. These were the professionals of Lubbock. Two members, as I recall, were principals of schools, another member worked at the Lubbock School District office as an administrator, employment workers, an airline pilot and several school teachers. Most of the members had well paying jobs and drove nice cars.

This small church was very faithful in Sunday School, Bible study, prayer meetings, choir practice and worship services. You could always count on them to be in the right place at the right time.

Mt. Vernon United Methodist Church believed in helping the needy. We had a food pantry at the church and people would come by the church to pick up sacks of non-perishable items. It was wonderful to see the church members helping the less fortunate. They loved what they were doing and I was a proud pastor.

One evening in the middle of our Bible study, some man called from a local motel and wanted to talk to me. He and his wife and two small children were coming from somewhere I can't remember, but their car had stopped about 30 miles back. He said they had run out of gas and there were no service stations around. They had not had anything to eat all day and they were starving. They did not have any money, so they were in need of money and food. I told the class about this situation.

We prayed fervently, got up to fix hot dogs we always kept on hand at the church. A couple of ladies went home and brought back oranges, bananas, apples, grapes, cookies, potato chips and suckers for the kids. Would you believe that starving people would not take a bite of anything, not even the two small kids? We asked them a few questions and their answers came back a little differently. We knew then they were lying. I offered to take them back to their car in my car. They did not want to do that because a friend of theirs was going to pick them up after he got off work at 11:00 pm. The more we asked them questions, the more they lied. We stayed there about 30 minutes, and the food was never tasted. We left the food with them. I'm shaking my head now thinking how some people will try to fool you to get a dollar. I learned that night to be very careful. Ephesians 5:15-16 says it this way. "See then that you walk circumspectly, not as fools, but as wise. Redeeming the time, because the days are evil."

Shortly after this encounter, a beggar dressed up like a bishop came by the church. He had a black turban around his head, a white clergy collar around his neck, a long black preacher's robe and polished laced up black boots. He came to see me for some money to buy gas for his car. These types of people always come around at the very beginning of a worship service. They are good at it! They do it all the time. I told him I couldn't help him, so I sent a couple of men to check on him. I think one of the men gave him $10.00. I also keep learning that when you try to do good, evil is always present. So—watch out!

I remember Tommy Braxton, Jr., son of JT and Bernice used to come to Lubbock bringing his alto and tenor saxophones and his soprano clarinet. He and his father often played a medley of songs together. They could really play, and the church was really blessed every time he came to Lubbock.

Most of the time, Tommy would notify us when he was coming to Lubbock. Most of the churches were notified, and out little church had only standing room when he came. He certainly is a talented musician who writes his own lyrics and has cut a few CD's.

In 1988 Collin and Chanta'l came to Lubbock, TX to live with us. It was a blessing for my wife and me to do this while Collin pursued his education. Leaving Chanta'l with us after he graduated, she became my little girl for the next several years. A blessing to be sure.

She was very sprightly, very lively, always wanting to do something or to go somewhere. This was an everyday occurrence. Her favorite establishment was Dairy Queen; she loved their ice-cream bars.

We would always stop at a park on our way home or at a grocery store. She would love to roam around the store while I shopped. Sometimes I didn't know where she was! She was reprimanded for this on a number of occasions! She was not a bad girl by any means; she just liked to go! go! go! And go some more!

When evening came after supper, she was tired and exhausted from her daily activities. She was fun to be around. Then, I would say, OK, Chanta'l, it is time to go to bed." She would say, "Grandpa, read me one more story". I did, and sometimes she would fall asleep in my arms. I would say, "Good night, Chanta'l." She would say, "Good night, Grandpa." What a memoir! What a blessing this was to help raise a child of 1-2 years of age to about 7-8 years of age. We enjoyed it!! She did too! What a blessing!

I stayed in Lubbock for five years at the Mt. Vernon United Methodist Church. Many of the members have now gone on to be with the Lord, and I know they are rejoicing in heaven. I think of them from time to time. They were such sweet people, lovable to me and my family. I will never forget all of the wonderful people there.

Well, it is time to pack up again, for life still goes on! We moved to Abilene, Texas in 1993 to Grace United Methodist Church, which had over 100 members. This was an all-white church, but that did not matter to me. White people need Jesus just like anybody else. Several families stopped coming to the church when they heard a Black pastor was coming. Can you believe it?

One member told me when I first got to the church that the Dallas Cowboys came on TV at 12:00 noon, and if I wasn't finished with my sermon by that time, several of the members would get up and leave. That did not matter to me either, for I never shortened God's Word for a few religious folks.

I tried to get Bible studies and prayer meetings started, but I never could successfully get them off the ground. I was devastated and heart-brokened and began to question God again. This church was a difficult situation for me for whatever reason. I tried my best to come up with the right messages to help the people, but seemingly, God's words fell on deaf ears. Life still goes on!

There were some very good people in this church, but I could not get them moving in the right directions. I'm not blaming them by any stretch of the imagination; it could have been me, I don't know.

Several of the leaders believed that they were working out their salvation by planting flowers, trimming the hedges and washing the windows. If it is true that people would work around and in the church to keep it clean and nice looking but people do not do that kind of work just to get to heaven. Ephesians 2:8-9 says, "For by grace are you saved through faith; and that not of yourselves; it is the gift of God. Not of works, lest any man should boast."

I looked out of my parsonage window one Saturday morning and noticed several people over at the church pulling weeds, raking leaves, pruning the rose bushes and washing the inside and outside windows. I walked over to congratulate them on what they were doing. They were busy as a bumble bee. One member told me quite frankly that they were working out their salvation, but that never mattered to me either one way or the other.

I just kept on preaching an uncompromising unadulterated gospel from God, and that was what I was supposed to do by God's grace.

Chanta'l had finished kindergarten and first grade in Abilene by this time. It was the year 1995, and I was getting ready to pack up again.

This time I was moving to Roswell, New Mexico to pastor another all white congregation.

Chanta'l's parents came to pick her up and take her back to Dallas. She was 7-8 years old by how. It was time again to say, "Good-bye".

As I am writing now thinking about the last 40 years of my life, I have said a lot of hellos and good-byes. My name should have been Hello-Goodbye (smile). Seriously, I have learned a lot of wonderful experiences as I traveled here and there and over yonder. Those of you who have traveled a lot have learned a lot by that experience.

I thank God for my experiences, some perhaps, unbelievable to some, nevertheless, true. The road has been very difficult at times, but God never said that the road would be easy.

The road of life is not a bed of roses. Someone said that "life is what you make of it." That's very true; life can be beautiful if we trust God to work out all things.

One experience at Grace United Methodist Church really hurt me deeply. There was a lady who died while I was pastor of this church. We were very close as brothers and sisters in the Lord. She was a very faithful woman who came faithfully to Bible Study and Prayer meetings. Sometimes we would be the only two meeting for prayer. I wanted so desperately to do her funeral eulogy.

Her family lived in another state, and they contacted the former pastor to do the funeral service. I was very discouraged, but "Life Still Goes On!"

I also remember packing the truck for our move to Roswell, NM. A couple of members came over I thought to help me load the truck. They just looked!! They just watched!! I still shake my head sometimes; they did not help me!! They did not offer to help me!

Well, the truck all packed by my wife and me, we headed toward Roswell, NM about four (4) hours away. We had a nice trip!! A member of Aldersgate United Methodist Church met us as we entered the city of 50,000 people and led us to our home.

It was a very nice three bedroom house, two bathrooms, a large kitchen, one-car garage and a huge brick walled back yard with a couple of peach trees. It was really nice. The neighbor across the street helped me unload the truck; the neighbor to the right of us brought us a six pack of coke. The neighbors on the left never said a word to us for 6 months or more. Oh well, I suppose they were waiting to see what kind of neighbors we would be or whatever. There were no other African Americans on this street but that's another matter that did not bother me. It bothered them, but that was their problem.

The next day we went to see the church, a couple of miles from our house. It did not look like an ordinary church building. There was an emblem or symbol on a high pole in front of the church, so I knew that this was the church on the corner of W. 19th Street and Union. It was a large church with a few classrooms, large fellowship hall, a large kitchen and the sanctuary was large also with carpet throughout. It was very nice. Several members of the church were there to greet us. This was a nice welcome to this all white church. Again, just like Abilene, a few members stopped coming when they heard that the new African American pastor had just arrived. I said to myself, "No, not again, not again". To this day in 1995, I still cannot figure out why some whites think that Blacks are so inferior.

Most of the congregation of about 100 members was very nice. Most of them treated me with respect and most of them were of the senior citizen age, 60 and over. There were only 2 or 3 middle-age people and only 1 or 2 teenagers. I thought from the very beginning that the church needed some more young people.

I continued a Bible study that was already in progress at the church beginning at one o'clock in the afternoons on Wednesdays. There were about 20 faithful members who were very opened to the study of God's Word. I was very happy to have a nice Bible study. The faithful members were: Jan Feick, Mona Smith, Muriel Foster, Edith Baird, Al Atkinson, Lois Bedford, Ginger Bissey, Sue Chesher, Callie Chrisman, Richard Cibak, and Mari, Connie Ozbun, Nita Goe, Ivan Hawkinson, Shirley Taylor, Roberta Loy, Sarah Wolfram, Susan Rennie, Louis Hunt, Mildred Price, Helen Bergmark and Billie Proctor. There were others, I'm sure, but names have a way of leaving my mind sometimes (smile). Several of these same people attended prayer meetings on Wednesday evenings. This was a far cry from the church in Abilene, Texas.

We had a nice choir led by Brad Bullock. He was really a good director of voice. He had all the sopranos, tenors, altos, and bases really singing wonderfully together.

After about six months, the Lord started adding members to the church, mostly young adults and some teenagers. The church was really growing by leaps and bounds. There were so many faithful elderly members who had gone on to be with the Lord. We needed new members. The Lord blessed in a mighty way!! Middle-age married adults started joining! Larry and Dixie Loy. Mike and Dollie McCowan.

Two of the most faithful members that I will always remember were Edith Baird and Dale Staten, both with the Lord now. Edith was over the music, rummage and bake sales and the Christmas bazaars. She was really a dedicated and faithful Christian. She died on my birthday, January 10, 2011. She will be greatly missed at the church. I preached her funeral!

Dale Staten passed away in 2010. He was the maintenance man, who took care of anything that broke down. He kept the lawn mowed and edged to perfection. He loved what he could do for the church. There were many others, too, who worked tediously in the church itself. I still have a 1996 church directory that I pick up occasionally and thumb through. Most of them have seen each other in heaven rejoicing with each other. I'm glad about that!!

Oh yeah!! My next door neighbors to the left of us began inviting us over to their house for barbecue. Time does bring about a change. We ended up being happy neighbors!!

Again, it was difficult to say good-bye to this faithful church, but I was getting a little tired at 69 years of age. In the United Methodist, pastors had to retire at age 70, but I retired a year early and accepted a part-time pastorate position at Mackey Chapel United Methodist Church in Odessa, Texas, some 200 miles back east of Roswell, New Mexico. This was to be a one year assignment, and then I was to retire for good!!

Mackey Chapel United Methodist Church, a small African American church of less than 100 members, was, in my estimation, the most spiritual churches during my tenure as pastor.

I remember one Sunday was lay Sunday when the lay members took over the morning service. I was so proud of them that Sunday morning as brother Keith Thompson led the service. He spoke briefly and did he speak!! He surprised me, but when the Lord leads a person, you never know what will happen. Other members spoke as well. At the end of the service, we all gathered around in front of the church, held hands together, prayed and cried joyfully. It was a service to be remembered, and oh how well I do? It was awesome! The Lord was really lifted up that day!! What a memoir!!

I haven't kept in touch with any member since I left in 2000, but I do remember our piano player and director of the choir, Sis Frizella Whitaker. She could really "whip" those keys and sing, too. She would come to the church early every Sunday morning and start playing and singing. Sometimes, she would be at the church before I arrived. I could hear her playing and singing when I walked into the church. What a blessing that was to me!!

Every now and then, brother and sister Wilmer Ray would invite everyone over to their house for barbecue, hotdogs and hamburgers. They really enjoyed doing this!!

I remember one morning, I dropped a paper clip on the floor, reached down to pick it up and I could not get up. I had to crawl to the bathroom. I went to a chiropractor in Odessa for several months. After the treatment, I felt worse than I did when I went. Finally, I went to a back specialist, who sent me to his assistant who was an African American. He examined me thoroughly and prescribed some pain pills for me. They did not help! I had a sciatic nerve disorder in my back and sometimes the pain would go down my right thigh to my ankle and boy it sure did hurt. I had to use a cane periodically and sometimes I had to preach sitting down. I was really hurting at times, not all of the time, but the pain would hit me when I least expected it.

That is the way life is most of the time. Certain situations happen to us when we had no idea that they were coming at us, sometimes faster than a speeding bullet.

I went back to the Black doctor who told me that I needed to have an MRI at the hospital. I did, and they have yet to tell me what was wrong or what I needed to do. While I am still thinking about that experience, I cannot understand for the life of me why this Anglo back specialist sent me to his assistant? Oh well—

Life still goes on!!

My family came down from Texas to see me at this time. I had my cane nearby in case I had to use it. Their visit seemed to have helped me have less pain and did not have to use my cane very often. We prayed thanking God together and they drove back to Dallas. The pain was subsiding now in my somewhat weary state, but I happened to turn to Paul's epistle to the church at Galatia when he says, "And let us not be weary in well doing: for in due season we shall reap, if we faint not, (Galatians 6:9).

It seemed to me the Lord was saying, "Get up, Curtis, quit feeling sorry for yourself!" I got up and drove to Roswell, NM, where I had known a Christian chiropractor for many years. I went to see him, told him what I had been going through for several months. He listened and listened and pretty soon he started praying. He prayed I know for a solid 30 minutes without stopping. I have never in my 71 years of living heard anybody pray like he did. I was kind of wondering myself why he was praying so long? Then I read where James says in James 5:16, "The fervent prayer of a righteous man availeth much". I'm shaking my head now thinking about that long prayer.

He then shot me which sounded like bullets coming from a 50 caliber machine gun all over my back and down my legs. It was a little scary hearing all that noise, but I knew that he knew what he was doing. He said, "You can get up now."

I felt like the impotent man in John 5:8 when Jesus told him to "Rise, take up your bed and walk." He was made whole that day at the pool of Bethesda and so was I. My back has not bothered me since, and that has been over 10 years ago. Someone says, "God is good all the time, all the time God is good!"

I went back to Odessa to finish up my year. My wife had gone to Dallas to look for an apartment or house in that area, so we could be closer to our two sons, Curtis Jr. and Collin.

CHAPTER TWELVE
THE END OF THE JOURNEY

My wife would come back to Odessa periodically to see me and the members of the Mackey Chapel. We were happy to see each other after several weeks. She enjoyed spending time with our two sons and other members of the family. I was looking forward to moving to Dallas after retiring for good, but what we planned did not come to fruition. The Lord does work in mysterious ways, His wonders to perform.

I am 70 years of age at this time, and I have had a very interesting and amazing life as you could tell by reading my story. The challenges, opportunities and the many wonderful experiences have helped me to realize that life is worth living. It gets rough sometimes climbing upon the rough side of the mountain, but if we hold on to the hand of Jesus, the one who brought us out of sin and shame, He will pull us up! He will make a way out of no way; He will make the rugged path seem smooth and straight; He will turn a crisis into an opportunity; He will make all of our troubles, heart-aches and pains become a joy, if we trust Him!

One song-writer wrote:

> "I trust in God, wherever I may be,
> Upon the land or on the rolling sea.
> Oh come what may, from day to day,
> My heavenly Father watches over me."

When my wife would come back to Odessa for a few days, we sometimes would talk about our first meeting each other. It was love at first sight! We reminisced about the street dances on Stueben Street we used to have from time to time. She was really a good dancer, and could jitterbug, too. We even talked about our old ex-boyfriends and ex-girlfriends. We would just laugh about that small matter. She would go back to Dallas to search for a place to live when I retired from Mackey Chapel for good. I was excited about moving back to Dallas to be closer to family and friends.

I continued to preach at the church in Odessa. I'm standing up now, I did not have to sit in a chair or sit on a stool to preach! This certainly was a blessing from the Lord! Mackey Chapel was a praying church. The members could really call on Jesus in prayer! We prayed for my retirement, we prayed that my wife would find an affordable place for us to live, we prayed for the church to grow numerically and we prayed for everybody near and far. This was the only church I pastored to have intense and spirited prayer meetings. It was exciting for the dozens of people who attended regularly.

My wife would come back to Odessa, and we would talk about that same old ex-boyfriend, ex-girlfriend phenomenon. I don't know why. I guess it was my inquisiveness or, perhaps, it could have been the malice in me, I don't know. I have always been a persistent person. I remember my Speech coaching; it was always practice! practice! practice!!

If you want to win first place, you've got to practice and practice and practice some more! That was one of the reason the speech students did so well. Practice does not make perfect, but it makes for perfection!

My wife would come back to Odessa, and it was the same old story over again. She did not want to talk about our old ex-boyfriends or ex-girlfriends. Sometimes she would get very upset and run upstairs. I could not understand why she got so upset. I suppose it was constant persistence on my part. I know from God's word in Philippians 3:13, "To forget those things which are behind, and reaching forth unto those things which are before." I could not forget the one issue that stood between us. She finally found a nice apartment for us, but it was a little too late now. In my hasty decision, I filed for a divorce which was granted in the year 2000, just a couple of years from celebrating our 50th year in marriage!

What suffering and shame this has caused me and my family? My own children and many of my relatives have not said anything to me in several years. I have talked to many of them recently and prayerfully, we are coming around to be what we are supposed to be and that is One Big Happy Family!! At lease, in Christ Jesus!

I remember reading about Abraham, Isaac, Jacob, Joseph and especially Job. Job lost everything, his children, all of his money; he even lost his health. In all of this, he never cursed God; God simply led him to have more faith, even though he suffered greatly. There are many biblical men and women who have suffered greatly, but that did not stop a Ruth or Esther or Naomi. I think of Jesus Christ who suffered for the whole world when He was crucified on that old rugged cross. So, count your blessings and see what the Lord has done in our life and how He brought us out of the pig pen to where we are today. I thank God for His deliverance, but once again, I was again saying, "Good-bye," this time, not to students, not to church members, not to friends, but to the Only Girl That I Have Ever Truly Loved!!! That's a fact!!

I finally retired and became a fugitive much like Moses in Exodus Chapter 3. I moved to Kansas City, Missouri; Wichita, Kansas and Des Moines, Iowa. I felt somewhat like the Apostle Paul when God sent him to Arabia instead of Jerusalem. This was good for Paul, however, because he was all alone, isolated in the desert. All he could think about was his encounter and call to the ministry on the road to Damascus (Galatians 1:17, Acts 9).

I had time now to do nothing but think about my past life. It was an enjoyable, fruitful life, but a sinful life as well (Romans 3:23). I had previously been troubled on every side, yet not in distress, perplexed, but not in despair, persecuted, but not forsaken; cast down, but not destroyed; (2nd Corinthians 4:8-9). God still loves me unconditionally even when I was a sinful man, but life still goes on! Life still goes on!!

While in Kansas City, my immediate family came from Texas to visit my sister, Pearline, who was still unable to walk, but still very cheerful.

I tried desperately to compose myself, to relax and enjoy their company. I tried to fit in the best way I knew how, but I could tell by the look on their faces that they were not too happy about seeing me. I felt so aloof, so alone from the only family I ever knew, from the family I love dearly and still do. In 2003, I had re-married!! Again, I was saying "good-bye" to my immediate family. I did not know that it would be over 7 years before I heard from any of them.

My second wife and I left each other temporarily. She went to Des Moines, Iowa to be closer to her 3 sisters, and her mother who was in a nursing home. I went to Wichita, Kansas to be closer to my ex-mother-in-law, brother and sister in-law Willie and Frankie McPherson.

My ex-wife had moved from Texas to Wichita to take care of her ailing mother. I worked at 3 jobs while I was in Wichita. I was weary, weak and worn, but I had a little time to rest, relax, pay bills, go to church and visit my ex-wife every now and then.

While in Wichita, some of my immediate family and some from Arizona and some of my nieces and a nephew came from California to see their grandma who was on her way to be with the Lord. It was just a matter of time. It was good to see my 3 nieces and nephew whom I had not seen in 10 to 15 years. Some looked at me as if to say, "What have you done?" "Why did you do what you did?" Some of my family thought that I was demon possessed. What a memoir?! Unbelievable!!

I had the opportunity to talk with them individually. Some believed my story, some did not. Again, I said "good-bye" as they returned home.

I tried my earnest to reconcile with my ex-wife that one issue that separated us, but to no avail. We could not come to an agreement!! We could not!! We would not! I tried in vain for reconciliation, but it did not work out; it just did not work out. It is now water under the bridge; it is all over, it is all over, but life still goes on until Jesus calls us all home to be with Him forever.

I would like to say that I love all of you deeply and dearly and hope and pray to see each one of you on this side of the Jordan River. Please forgive and forget any wrong doing I have or anyone else has done. The following scriptures speak to that fact: (Ex. 32:32, Ps. 86:5, Jer. 31:34, Matt. 9:6, Luke 6:37, and Ps. 77:9). There are many more scriptures on forgiveness. Eph. 3:20 sums it up this way, "Now unto Him that is able to do exceeding abundantly above all that we can ask or think according to the power that worketh in us.

And to my 8 grandchildren, keep the fire going and the ripples rippling as you reach your highest heights, educationally. I thank God from where you were to where you are today. My children's children are next!!

Janice' children: David Sr. is writing his first book!

1. David Almond, Jr. pursuing his BA degree at the University of California in Riverside, CA.

2. Monica Almond, presently working on her PhD degree at the Claremont Graduate School in Claremont, CA.
3. Timothy Almond, recently graduated from the University of California in Riverside, CA. with a BA degree.
4. Eric Almond will begin his college career soon.

Curtis' children:

1. Brian Hayes, a graduate of the University of Texas in Arlington, Texas. BA degree.
2. Myra Hayes, a graduate of the University of Texas in Arlington, Texas. BA degree.
3. Curtis the third is also a graduate of the University of Texas in Arlington, Texas. BA degree.

Collin's children:

1. Chanta'l Hayes, a graduate of DePaul University in Chicago, IL. BA degree.

All of my 8 grandchildren are now working, doing well and will pursue their Master's degree when God says, "Go, Go get it!"

And to all of my 9 great grandchildren, keep the ripples rippling as your parents have done, and may God bless each of you!!

EPILOGUE

As I look hindsight now, I can say with assurance that I am very proud of my family with all of their accomplishments. I tried my best to instill within each of them education is one of the keys to being successful. It has worked out!!

I made the best possible home for them when they were growing up. My teaching experience made that come true. I desperately wanted that to happen and it did by God's grace. I believe I was a good father to each of them. I even worked two jobs for a long time to make sure my finances would enable me to sacrifice everything I had just for them. I would do it all over again.

I have not always been a good husband, but I was a good father to my three children. They even know that too! Life Still Goes On regardless of whatever happens to anyone in this fleeting life.

One song-writer wrote:

> *"If when you give the best of you service, telling the world that the Saviour has come. Be not dismayed when men don't believe you, He'll understand and say, "Well-Done!"*
>
> Excerpt from song "He'll Understand!"

ACKNOWLEDGMENTS

I want to thank God, first of all, who inspired me to write my life story, "Life Still Goes On."

I want to thank my mother and father, both of whom went to be with the Lord in 1982. Their dedication and perseverance to instill the desire in their children to stay in school and study hard was uppermost in their endeavors.

I want to thank my brother, Otis, who always advised me to write without malice in my heart—Thanks Otis, for helping me to accentuate the positives and eliminate the negatives.

I want to thank Pastors Floyd E. Brown, Eddie B. Lane, and Gerald Fonte who supported me financially when I was a missionary in Liberia, W. Africa.

Thanks to Larry Mahan, a close friend of mine for fifty years, who taught the same time I did in the 60's at Franklin Junior High School. He and his wife, Donna typed the first draft of my manuscript. Thanks Larry and Donna.

To all of my students, while substituting in the Roswell Independent School District, to tell me to hurry up and finish your book so they could read it!!

And last but not least, my wife, Frances deserves a bunch of thanks for being patient with me while finishing the manuscript. Thanks Frances; I love you! We both trust that my life story will help and bless at least one person.

Sincerely,

Curtis L. Hayes

PS. Thanks Bianca, my final typist, who submitted it to my publisher.